Opals
of the
Never Never

Opals
of the
Never Never
Revised Edition

Robert G. Haill

Kangaroo Press

Acknowledgments

Special thanks to Bruno Resignano, Information Resources, South Australian Department of Mines and Energy, who personally selected colour transparencies from the archives and gave me considerable help with research.

Special thanks to Barrie O'Leary, honorary president of the Opal Society of Australia for his kind help and permission to use extracts from his book *A Field Guide to Australian Opals*.

Peter Caust, Underground Books, Coober Pedy, for his valuable assistance and most of the photos used in this book, taken by himself as a professional photographer.

Mr Altmann and Mr Cherney of Altmann and Cherney gem merchants, for their colour photographs of their precious gem material and information on the *Olympic Australis* belonging to them. The excellent photographs were taken by Rick Altmann.

The generous assistance of the South Australian Tourist Department in giving their permission to use information on climatic conditions, local facilities, fauna and flora and tourist statistics.

The publicity branch of the South Australian Premier's Department for their guide to the Opal Fields of South Australia.

The collective departments, Department of Interior, Division of National Mapping, Department of Minerals and Energy, for their topographic and geological information.

Above all the painstaking efforts of a fellow writer, my father, in editing and offering assistance in compiling and preparing the manuscript for the publishers.

And that wonderful gal, Shirley Hodges, who put her heart and soul into the effort of gathering and checking the facts, without complaint. And ready to do it all over again.

All I can say is, thank you all.

© Robert G. Haill 1981 and 1995

First published in 1981
This revised edition first published by Kangaroo Press Pty Ltd in 1995
3 Whitehall Road Kenthurst NSW 2156 Australia
PO Box 6125 Dural Delivery Centre NSW 2158
Printed in Hong Kong through Colorcraft Ltd

ISBN 0 86417 686 4

Contents

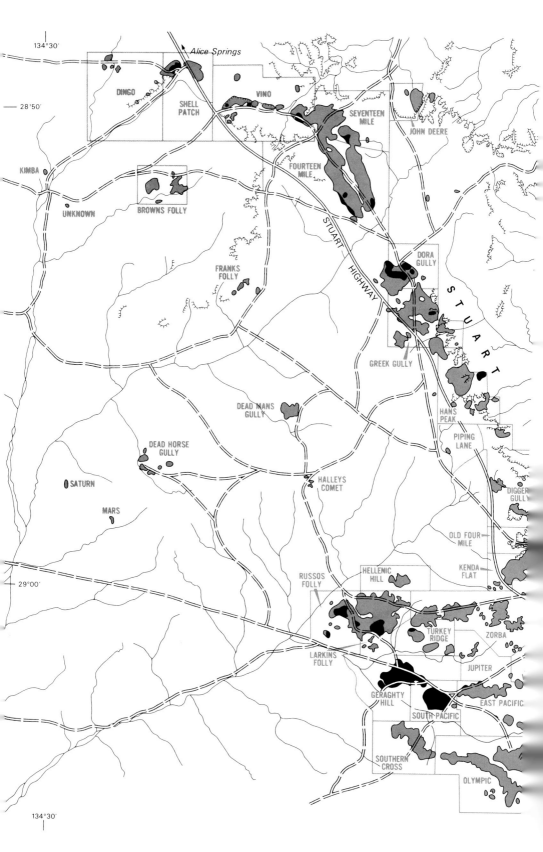

134°30'

← Alice Springs

134°30'

28°50'

29°00'

DINGO

SHELL PATCH

VINO

SEVENTEEN MILE

JOHN DEERE

KIMBA

UNKNOWN

BROWNS FOLLY

FOURTEEN MILE

STUART HIGHWAY

DORA GULLY

S T U A R T

FRANKS FOLLY

GREEK GULLY

DEAD MANS GULLY

HANS PEAK

DEAD HORSE GULLY

PIPING LANE

SATURN

DIGGER GULLY

MARS

HALLEYS COMET

OLD FOUR MILE

KENDA FLAT

RUSSOS FOLLY

HELLENIC HILL

LARKINS FOLLY

TURKEY RIDGE

ZORBA

JUPITER

GERAGHTY HILL

SOUTH PACIFIC

EAST PACIFIC

SOUTHERN CROSS

OLYMPIC

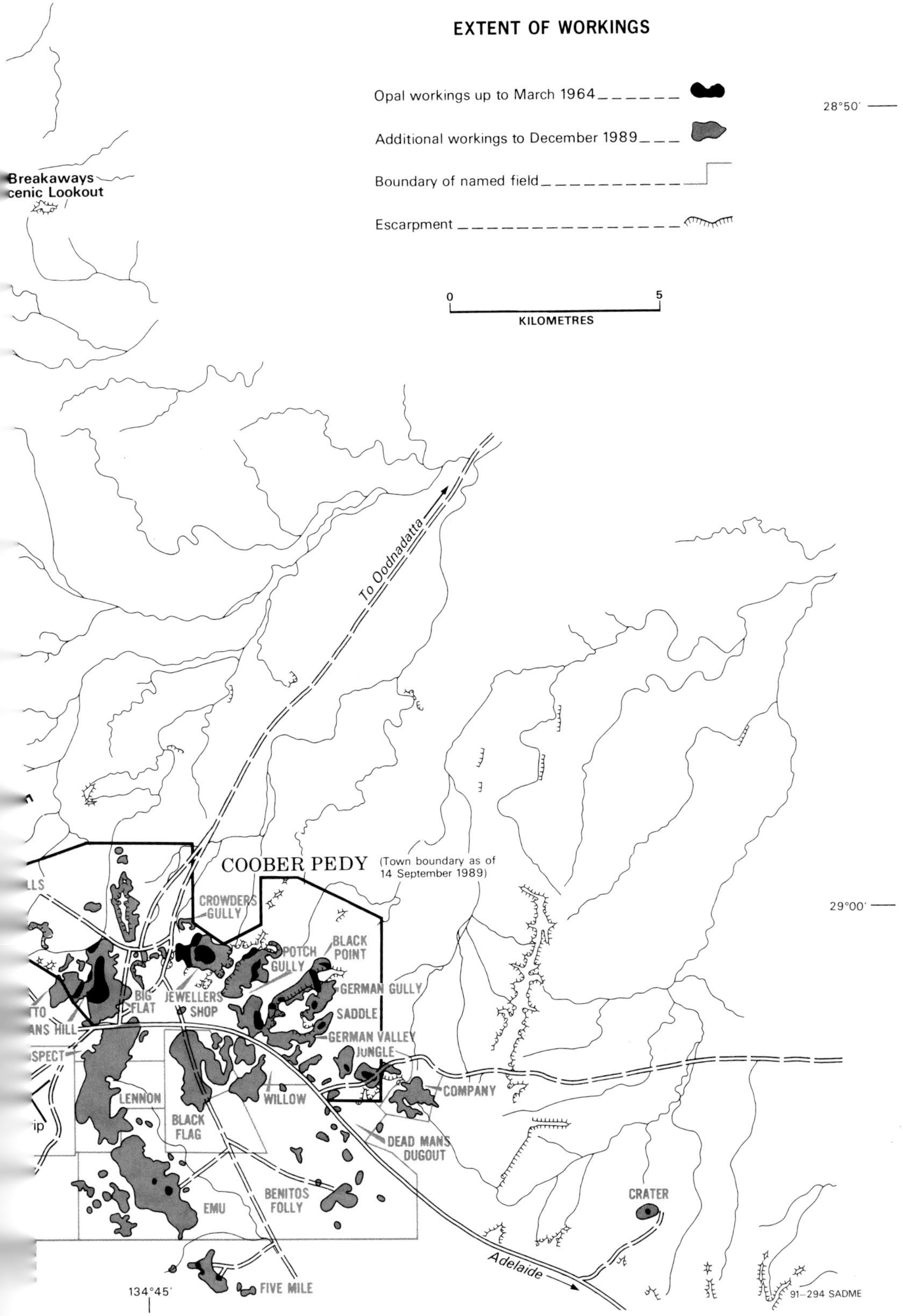

EXTENT OF WORKINGS

Opal workings up to March 1964 _ _ _ _ _ _

Additional workings to December 1989_ _ _

Boundary of named field _ _ _ _ _ _ _ _ _

Escarpment _ _ _ _ _ _ _ _ _ _ _ _ _ _

28°50'

0   5

KILOMETRES

Breakaways
cenic Lookout

To Oodnadatta

COOBER PEDY (Town boundary as of
14 September 1989)

29°00'

CROWDERS
GULLY

BLACK
POINT

POTCH
GULLY

GERMAN GULLY

SADDLE

BIG
FLAT

JEWELLERS
SHOP

GERMAN VALLEY

JUNGLE

LLS

TO
ANS HILL

SPECT

COMPANY

LENNON

WILLOW

DEAD MANS
DUGOUT

rip

BLACK
FLAG

CRATER

EMU

BENITOS
FOLLY

Adelaide

134°45'

FIVE MILE

91-294 SADME

Foreword

Coober Pedy. A name. Two little words. But Coober Pedy is an outback Australian town that has sustained a mineral rush for 80 years continuously. A race for precious opal, Australia's national gemstone.

More valuable than gold, Coober Pedy's quality opal is worth up to $5000 per ounce—in its rough state, as it is dug from the ground.

Australia supplies the jewellery trade of the whole world with opal, and Coober Pedy produces the bulk of all that. We cannot imagine the thousands, millions even, of opals that Coober Pedy produces every year.

Coober Pedy. It excites my imagination. It holds the lure of fabulous treasures and untold wealth locked away and buried in the earth. But whereabouts? Where exactly in the ground? And how can we find out? Just who could we ask? *They* ought to write a book about it!

That is just what Bob Haill has now completed and you can read it for yourself. It is all in here; everything that you wanted to know about Coober Pedy and couldn't find anyone to ask!

As you move through this book you are physically escorted through Coober Pedy. You are at its discovery and you are finding chips on the dumps. The photographic coverage shows the town and the mines. It brings out the humanity of the townspeople and reveals some startling aspects of opal's unending varieties.

This book is a training ground. It certainly gives its reader the advantages of a complete pseudo-experience. And it is especially interesting and attractive to look at.

Congratulations, Bob, for your superb compliment to Australia's opal industry.

Barrie O'Leary
President
Opal Society of Australia
Sydney NSW

Preface

Since *Opals of the Never Never* was first published in 1981, there have been considerable improvements in road conditions and tourist facilities throughout the Far North of South Australia, especially in the region of Coober Pedy, and many fabulous opal finds have resulted from alternative mining procedures, important facts determining that a new edition of the opal book should be published.

The discovery of opal at Stuart Range (now Coober Pedy) in 1915 has lured many adventurous persons in search of fortunes and, indeed, many have gouged their millions from this parched, rugged, inhospitable outback area. Others have come and sweated and toiled in vain, leaving discouraged and sometimes bankrupt.

More valuable than gold, a matchbox full of precious opal (approximately 30 grams or one ounce) can fetch up to $10 000 in its rough state, as it is dug from the ground: double its worth of 15 years ago.

Australia supplies the jewellery trade of the whole world with opal, and Coober Pedy produces the bulk of that. We cannot imagine the many millions of opals that Coober Pedy produces every year as no realistic monitoring has been successfully devised. The wary, intrepid miners do not voice loudly their finds, for obvious reasons.

A visit to Coober Pedy's opal fields is surely one of the remaining great adventures on which one can embark. There is the thrill of walking the ground where untold millions of dollars of opal still lie undiscovered, of mingling with the colourful miners of every nation on earth and hearing their stories of Lady Luck and the New Chum tourist who picks up a precious opal which has lain so long waiting to be claimed out in The Land of a Thousand Gibbers.

Dreams and fantasies and reality weave a spell on all who come here, drawing them back again and again to unearth the secret hiding places of the opals in this Never Never land.

Robert G. Haill

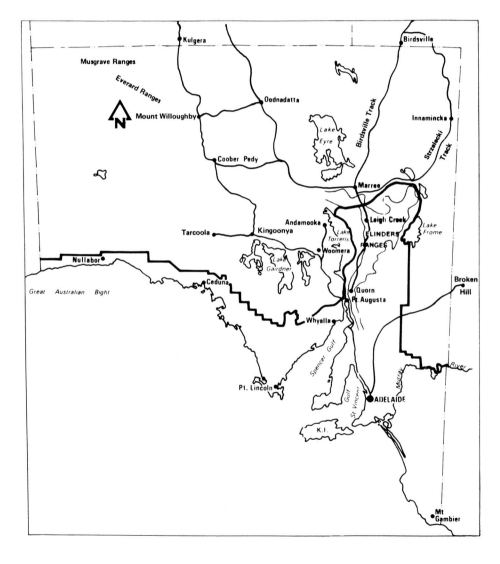

Map of South Australia. The heavy black line indicates the southern limits of the opal-bearing area of the state

1 *The birth of Coober Pedy*

It is a well documented fact that the majority of visitors to the Coober Pedy opal fields contract a mysterious, incurable disease known as Opalmania. This fever which recurs annually has easily recognised symptoms. Those afflicted have an uncontrollable urge to make a frenzied dash across thousands of kilometres to escape all civilisation and return to Coober Pedy. On arrival, armed with picks and shovels, they will rush insanely into the desert region beyond the town to dig and hack at the ground, often in 35°C heat, finally falling to their knees with wild cries to gather up fragmented chips of coloured rock. Doctors have given the common name of Fossicking to this terrible affliction. You have been warned.

I stated in an earlier edition of this book that there is a strange fascination about opal that creates a fever in people to search for it, and when they find it they surround individual pieces with myths and legends. Stories of famous name-stones being cursed and becoming harbingers of misfortune and death only enhance the attraction of these rare and precious gems; and I still hold to this.

Countless books have been written about opal and the colourful characters who spend a lifetime searching for it. These epic tales of hardship and violence in the vast arid regions capture the imagination and fire it with the thrill of adventure. The opal fields are portrayed as last frontiers where the law of the jungle still prevails.

My first trip to Coober Pedy was a number of years ago. I determined to set out to discover the opal fields for myself and to try my luck. Cautiously I sought for information that would tell me how to go about it properly. I wanted to know the conditions I should expect on my arrival. I intended to prospect and I wanted to be appropriately equipped. And if I were lucky enough to find opal, then where and how to sell it! The available books had no such information; they were, more or less, romantic yarns or geological textbooks that didn't help me. Nonetheless I set off in an old Volkswagen Kombi van, taking with me every conceivable thing that I thought could be useful, for want of any previous information.

I chose Coober Pedy to visit as at that time it was producing 90 per cent of the world's opal, and I set off on my adventure from Melbourne in fine spirits. Before I arrived I had to coax the Kombi over hundreds of kilometres of badly corrugated road, reconciled to leaving civilisation behind. How different nowadays with the fine bitumined highway that gives visitors to this region such a comfortable ride.

When I finally arrived my disillusionment would beggar description: Coober Pedy was a thriving modern township with every civilised amenity—there was even a drive-in theatre. There were none of the expected humble 'general stores', instead there were grand emporiums selling everything from a fish hook to a bulldozer. And I had brought half a tonne of tinned food, mining equipment and water for 1700 kilometres over almost impossible ground!

Thankfully I found the town was only a tourist facade. Motoring out onto the opal fields I discovered the area lived up to my fullest expectations. It was hungry and desolate and Spartan; men slaved to gouge the precious stone from the ground. On my most recent visit I found these conditions had not changed.

Opals of the Never Never is not an armchair adventure story. It is a lay person's guide to opal mining. Suffer the extremes of desiccating heat, the wet, the snakes and scorpions if you will, there is opal galore and adventure untold—if you know where and how to find it. That and the peace of the outback. The homely atmosphere of the oil-lit huts on the fields, the flickering of camp fires illuminating the white hills of the diggings creates an impression of time standing still in Coober Pedy.

If it wasn't for a fourteen-year-old boy, Bill Hutchinson, accompanying his father on a gold-seeking expedition and finding opal by chance while searching for water, Coober Pedy might not have been established initially as the richest opal-bearing region in the world.

On 6 February 1915 a party of four left Naracoorte to locate quartz reefs between Anna Creek and Coolgardie. Heading north the group was hampered by a severe drought and the urgent need to find water for themselves and their camels. Many days were spent in an unsuccessful search for water as they headed into the inhospitable Stuart Range. The heat was severe, registering between 46° and 51°C in the shade and the party split up, going in different directions to give themselves every chance of finding water.

One morning young Bill Hutchinson was left in charge of the camp while the others continued their search. When they returned at dusk they found that he had disappeared. As the fire was out and the ashes cold, it appeared he had been away for several hours. There was no hope of finding the boy's tracks in the darkness so a fire was lit with the intention of searching for him at daylight. It was hoped he might see the fire which would direct him back to the camp if he wasn't too far away.

As the last glimmer of light left the sky the boy strolled back to the camp and threw down a sugar-bag saying, 'Here, will you look at this—I think it's opal.'

'What are you talking about? And why did you disobey my orders? I told you not to leave the camp. You could have got lost. We've troubles enough not having water without needing to search the bush for you.'

'But, Dad, I've found water. Plenty of it and enough to last a fortnight at least. But look in the bag. It's opal, I know it is.'

It was opal, and the lad had found water, but only sufficient to last for eight days. During this time the party gathered opal floaters and continued in vain to search for water. Finally they were compelled to return to Adelaide, arriving there on 28 March 1915.

The opal they had found was sent to T. C. Wollaston, Australia's best-known authority on opals. It turned out that the opal was worthless as it had crazed and bleached in the sun. But it did show that there were opal deposits in the Stuart Ranges.

The news travelled fast and several groups left Anna Creek to find the Hutchinson field. They searched for months with no luck. They lost their camels and the drought conditions still prevailed.

Then two brothers, Jim and Dick O'Neill, experienced opal miners from White Cliffs, heard the rumour of opal in a new field, a roadless 200 kilometres to the north, and decided to take the chance of finding it. The O'Neills set out on their journey with two horses and a spring dray. They struck their course by compass through mulga scrub and over sandhills for a distance of 97 kilometres in virtually a straight line and had water relayed to them through a chain of camel drivers.

After many hardships the O'Neills arrived at the Range and at exactly the place where Hutchinson's party had camped, but they decided it was not the actual field and they needed to press on further. With worn-out boots and calico to bind their bleeding feet they reached a place where the ground was covered with opal floaters and opal outcrops and they decided that here they would stay and mine.

The O'Neills stayed for nine months before returning with opal that Wollaston valued at £17 000: a fortune in those days. Wollaston took samples of this opal to America and quickly found buyers.

There was an exodus from White Cliffs and other opal fields with a rush to the 'new find'. Claims were staked as a trail was blazed across the arid Gibson Desert. Within four years Coober Pedy, as the Aborigines called it, had a population of nearly five hundred. They came from the Cliffs, the

Ridge, even from England to burrow into the hills and honeycomb the desert.

Some of them found thousands of ounces of opal in a single day and it flooded the market. Opal outstripped in production value all the other minerals in Australia, with the exception only of copper.

But still there was the lack of water. And often water was regarded as more precious than the finest opal. Even so, Coober Pedy came alive as the richest, fastest growing opal field in Australia.

In an attempt to overcome the water problem the Engineering and Water Supply Department set about the enormous task of installing a great circular concrete underwater tank at a cost of £8000. It was 100 metres in diameter and 4 metres deep, filled by the run-off from nearby slopes, and roofed with iron to stop evaporation and to prevent birds drowning in it. A fence was erected to keep out the wild animals. Now Coober Pedy had a regular supply of 2000 kilolitres of water.

With improved conditions, miners brought their families to the field and built secure and comfortable homes. A general store was established and law and order was maintained.

But too much opal was being found too fast and opal prices slumped. It was impossible to find a market for the huge output. Overseas markets were cultivated, the largest being Germany, and prices for opal improved.

Known officially as the Stuart Range Opal field for the first ten years of its existence, the town was renamed Coober Pedy in early 1925. And this name stayed.

As the field developed, so did its extent. By 1925 the length of the range over which opal had been discovered was 50 kilometres in a NW and SE direction and the width was greater than 3 kilometres. The estimate of available opal was measured in the tonne.

But by 1931 the effects of the economic recession had hit hard upon the demand for luxury goods. And opal was a luxury even though it was selling as cheaply as a shilling a pound. The men started leaving the field. By late 1931 only 83 men remained at Coober Pedy and many of these could only afford to stay because of their pensions, for opal was practically worthless.

Until the end of World War II the total output from the Coober Pedy field earned the miners less than £167 000. But by 1946 this figure had jumped by the staggering amount of nearly £74 000, stabilising there until 1955 and rapidly climbing ever since. By 1959 it was estimated that the field was producing £2 million worth of first-grade gemstone annually.

The miners swarmed back to the opal fields in their thousands, and stayed. Coober Pedy was finally established.

2 *Where is it?*

Coober Pedy lies in the centre of the Stuart Ranges in South Australia. The town is 592 kilometres by road north-northwest of Port Augusta and 200 kilometres north of Tarcoola. This rich opal field established in 1915 accounts for 90 per cent of the whole of Australian opal now being found.

Approaching the town there are low flat-topped hills of desert sandstone typical of opal country and countless white sandstone mullock dumps around shafts that plunge deep into the ground. These dumps flank the red ribbon of corrugated road leading into Coober Pedy.

This treeless country with its dry mulga creeks and endless plains is the Gibson Desert and everywhere there are gibber stones.

The Aboriginal definition of Coober Pedy is 'white man in a burrow', and that about sums it up. The miners—Greeks, Italians, Germans, Czechs, Yugoslavs, Poles, and a few Australians—live in dugouts to escape the heat, for in the summer the temperature soars to an uncomfortable 54°C. The Aborigines, those not living on the Reserve, live in humpies, wurleys and old abandoned cars. On the fields, the miners live in tin sheds, caravans or hastily erected sheds. The dwellings lack any normal comfort.

Many men have died in the inhospitable Gibson Desert. There is no water and no trees for shade. Unceasing wind and blinding dust storms are added discomforts. There are venomous snakes and deadly spiders to contend with.

Here is opal, and more still in the ground than ever came out of it. Shafts have to be sunk in virgin ground or old workings taken deeper to find the million-dollar fortunes.

There is opal everywhere. At the Big Flat and Gibber Hill, Larkin's Folly and on the Perfecto Field. Companies of men working The Follies and Dora's Gully are on top grade opal at less than twelve metres down. New finds have been established on Koska's Hill, Poverty Terrace and Museum, while the old workings on the East Pacific, Faggot's and The Craters are being mined on deeper levels. Before long the diamond drills will move out to Bolshevik Gully and The Craters to pincer a huge opal-bearing area that takes in Mockingbird Hill, The Jungle, New Ryan's, Potch Gully and Russo's

Folly. These fields were declared barren until a Greek geologist proved that there was a very deep opal level running right through them.

From Han's Peak can be seen thousands of sprawling mullock dumps and it would appear the ground has been disembowelled. But these mullock dumps will grow higher as the miners bore deeper and deeper through level after level of precious opal dirt.

'The opal will never run out', say the old miners. 'Coober Pedy and away to Mintabie, 400 kilometres to the north, is solid opal.'

The miners give their names to the fields where rich opal is found and those names remain: Ryan's Gully, Geraghty's Hill, Farmers, Paulo's Ridge, Flannery's Gully, Tinker's, and Libbie's Find. They are markers that say 'opal has been found here'. They are part of the romance that is Coober Pedy and are tabled with the South Australian Department of Mines and Energy as a permanent marker of an established opal run.

Humanity's dream of leaving a mark can truly be realised here on the opal fields. Not only is one's name immortalised to mark success, it is also given to any unique or magnificent opal that is found, such as Dunstan's, Barton's, and many, many others.

But what kind of a person is it who will go out to inhospitable, lonely wastes, in search of a fortune? Only a fool perhaps, for only 'fools go where angels fear to tread'.

Michael John Bresclini was this kind of a person, and when he told his friends he was sure there was good opal still to be found at Crowder's Gully they laughed at him, saying he was wasting his time since the field was worked out.

But Bresclini ignored them and took his camp to Crowder's Gully. He understood the area well for he had worked there with three companies before. None of them had found opal. This time he enlisted the aid of a field geologist as a share partner. They established that three levels prevailed, each being 1.5 metres apart. None of these levels carried opal. The lowest level resembled that of the plateau workings while the other two were only horizontal bedding plane partings of local disconformity. Bresclini knew that most of the opal from this locality was found in oblique joints of varying altitude in the zone between the two upper levels and that ironstone under-lain by yellow sandstone was always found below the actual opal level.

For five months Bresclini worked away, sinking shafts that were duffers. His partner gave up, but before leaving told Bresclini that opal would only be found in irregular isolated pockets, or where there were minor fault lines that would cause strong verticals.

Bresclini hacked his way through grey billy, often 3 metres thick. He found iron-stained verticals, but no opal.

'Give it up and come over to the Eleven Mile', said his friends.

But Bresclini was stubborn to the point of being pig-headed and he persisted at Crowder's Gully. He decided to ignore the fundamental rules of opal geology which dictated that when you struck ironstone underlain by yellow sandstone there was no more opal. He went into his deepest shaft — down twenty metres—and kept digging. He worked through the bleached sediments and impermeable claystone below the sandy bed and found numerous confusing fault lines running at random. None of them localised in opal. And then he was sinking into heavily silicified pink sandstone.

Down twenty-five metres he started to ask himself if he wasn't wasting his time. Another week, he promised himself, and then he'd join the others at the Eleven Mile where a rich strike was being worked.

Two more days and another metre down he noticed the ground was becoming more stable. There were strong verticals with traces of good colour and he put in a drive to follow them. They were wide and branchy and ran into thick seams of potch. Where there was potch there was opal. He worked with renewed interest.

By the flickering light of a candle fixed to the wall he suddenly saw the first red glint, a winking eye of opal. He dropped his pick and went to work with a penknife. The red eye opened out to a four centimetre seam—a seam of magnificent crystal opal.

Bresclini won a parcel of opal worth over $80 000 in his deep shaft and found many isolated pockets of opal within 18 metres of the shaft in the following five months.

Sometimes the run of the opal defies geological reckoning and the rule book can be thrown away. But if geology can be ignored geography cannot. Geographical information on the Coober Pedy fields is essential, and a person's life can depend on it.

3 *Geology of Coober Pedy*

The extensive opal mining area of Coober Pedy is situated on Stuart Range, an erosional scarp 6 to 28 metres high which constitutes the divide between two flat planes and their systems of surface drainage. This divide extends lineally from the eastern end of the Everard Range to the northern end of Lake Torrens, separating the basin of Lake Cadibarra-wirracanna from Lakes Woorong, Phillipson and Wirrida. These large silt-filled clay pans contain water for a short time after heavy rains but otherwise they are completely dry.

This area is part of the stony desert of Central Australia with sand deposits replaced by continuous gibber stone overlay. The central portion of Stuart Range, where the opal deposits lie, is a remnant of a great tableland composed of horizontal beds of sandstone and claystone that were deposited in Cretaceous time. These beds extend beyond the lower Cretaceous shales that form the impervious cap confining the water of the Great Australian Artesian Basin to the underlying sands. The sediments laid down in Cretaceous time have been elevated since the period of deposition and have been greatly affected by erosion. The tableland formed by their elevation has been dissected by the agents of erosion in a very irregular manner.

The surface of the tableland is strewn with a mantle of hard siliceous stones or 'gibbers' characteristic of the terrain. Many of these are round and others angular, and some are composed of chalcedony or porcelainite. Where cemented together these gibbers form a conglomerate.

Where the siliceous capping of stones on the outliers of the tablelands has been removed by erosion there remain rounded hillocks of red or white claystone. Excavations into the claystone show a system of small pipe-like branching veins filled with ferruginous clay.

This Cretaceous formation, commonly accepted as Desert Sandstone, extends far beyond the known limits of proven opal-bearing country suggesting that a vast amount of opal-bearing strata remains to be uncovered.

The escarpment has a serrated edge peculiar to its individual erosion and the Tableland peninsula extends out to the lower plain where deep dissection has led to the development of numerous mesas or breakaways. Erosion is retarded by a capping of hard silcrete, but once this is removed, destruction of the softer underlying rock is rapid.

Major opal deposits lie close to the main divide where its direction changes from north-westerly to westerly, coinciding with the junction of east and west subsidiary divides, and drainage is radial around the principal opal centres.

Observations of the general occurrence of opal make it apparent that all the sedimentary opal deposits in Australia occur within the pallid zone of the mature laterite profile developed on a continent-wide peneplain during Tertiary times.

The laterite profile of Coober Pedy is generally expressed by 0–4 metres of silcrete commonly called 'grey billy'. From 4 to 11 metres, bleached sediments containing iron-stained vertical pipes are encountered. The 11 to 40 metres pallid zone contains the opal levels. Further depths reveal blue shale and the unweathered sediments; once it was considered useless to go deeper, however more recent investigation has revealed ultra lower opal levels can be found.

The pipes within the bleached sediments are vermicular tubes filled with red-brown sandy clay within the pallid zone. They are of inorganic origin and a product of lateritisation. These vermicular tubes have also been found at Lightning Ridge and throughout the Queensland opal fields.

It is established beyond doubt that opal is a product of laterite profile formation. At every opal deposit a similar lithological sequence is present within the laterite profile and bedding is approximately horizontal. The opal is localised at the contact between a sandy bed and an underlying impermeable claystone, suggesting that water moving downward plays a role in opal formation. The opal formed at a time when a pronounced fall in the water table took place. Where trapped ground water accumulated an opal deposit was localised.

Opal around Coober Pedy is particularly localised where the levels have been depressed, accompanying faulting causing levels to be separated. From the bottom up these are known as 'bottom', 'main' and 'squibby'. The name 'main' is often restricted to the level carrying the opal lode.

Minor faults and joints commonly called 'slides' are associated with these levels and have an important effect on the opal level. The levels vary, running straight or in waves until the slide intrudes and can cause the level to drift up or down or away for as far as three metres.

Minor jointing can be parallel to the fault line with the joints extending upwards into verticals that often form considerable repositories of gem opal. Multiple faults can occur on a single level and where they intersect a thick body of opal is often found.

Larkin's Folly, the Eight Mile and Russo's opal fields are all prone to slides and fault lines and some of the finest opal ever found has come from these locations. The miners search industriously for minor faults and follow them assiduously through the different levels. The slides strike in all directions with vertical displacements forming undulations and troughs: these areas are especially favourable for the location of opal.

At Larkin's Folly the level-dips at slide contacts are as high as 15 degrees. The slides vary from place to place and opal usually occurs most abundantly in the area of maximum dip where the level is at its lowest elevation. The slides pre-date laterite profile formation and the stony tableland soils and have no discernible surface expression. Their indisputable control over opal localisation makes them an ideal target for exploration and geophysical surveys.

Geologically, Coober Pedy is an easy field for opal exploration as the ground runs true to form and once an understanding of slides and minor fault lines is gained much of the hard work of mining and removing masses of dirt is eliminated. Geological maps available from the Department of Mines and Energy clearly indicate slide locations where opal has been found. The employment of an opal consultant with a geological degree to conduct exploration into unproven areas is well warranted.

4 *What is opal?*

It is generally understood that opal is a milky-white precious stone with changing colours that beam and flash as the stone is slanted from one angle to another; because it is fifth on the scale of precious stones it is not considered to be a highly precious gem, but first-grade opal ranks with and often above diamonds, both in value and beauty.

It is important to understand exactly what opal is before buying it as an investment, and certainly before spending considerable money going to the opal fields to mine it.

Although its personal appeal has some influence on the price opal will be bought or sold for, many other factors are equally important. A good opal must be stable, not subject to crazing or cracking. Some opal isn't ready to leave the ground. It has all the presentation but it isn't yet seasoned and it can fall apart during polishing, or later, after it is set in jewellery and sold.

Only over the past fifteen years has the chemistry of opal really been understood and this has been brought about by the growing demand for this beautiful stone.

So what exactly is opal?

Opal is a hydrated silica with the chemical formula of $SiO_2.nH_2O$ (silicon dioxide). It has a hardness of $5\frac{1}{2}$ to $6\frac{1}{2}$ on the Mohs scale.

Opal is a true precious stone which occurs in many varied forms. It is amorphous silica with a water content varying from one to twenty per cent depending on the porosity and degree of hydration. Precious opal usually contains from six to ten per cent water.

Opal may be dull and valueless, in which case it is called common opal; only vividly-coloured opal qualifies as precious opal. Common opal occurs in abundance throughout the world. One form, found in association with opal of value, is called potch. 'Potch' is an interesting word, probably a miner's corruption of 'potsherd', or pot-shard, meaning a broken piece. Such material was called 'schnide' in the early days on the White Cliffs field. Since one variety, crockery-potch, has the appearance of broken pottery, it is quite feasible that 'potsherd' formed the basis of the new noun.

In colour, potch may be white, grey, black, amber; it may be honey-coloured, watery-clear or a mixture of these colours. Transparent amber potch is girasol, or fire opal. When exceptionally transparent and bright yellow this fire opal is called sun opal. Another potch variety is named after the magpie on account of the tonal intermixing of black and white.

It is a standing joke among miners on the fields that when they die their bones will turn to useless potch and should they be dug up in a million or so years they would most likely be used for the backing of precious opal. And there's the optimistic miner who feeds his chickens potch mixed with bran. He's still waiting for an opalised egg.

But good quality potch is not entirely valueless and is used widely in opal doublet manufacture. Hyalite is a glassy, clear potch and hydrophane is a potch which, when wet, shows a definite but weak play of colours.

About ninety-five per cent of opal from the opal fields is potch: only five per cent is of any value. Of this five per cent about ninety-five per cent is of mediocre grade, with only five per cent of real value. It is this small percentage—five per cent of five per cent—that constitutes the magnificent gem which we call precious opal. Any other opal showing a play of colour, but which is not equal in grade to the tops, is noble opal, as are girasol and hydrophane.

It must be understood that this precious opal classification refers only to rough opal from which solid stones can be cut, or to finished gems which are solid stones. Top grade doublets or triplets are classified as noble opal, not precious, because their opal content is a veneer.

Solid opal is opal which is of natural occurrence and solid enough to be set as a gem. Any pieces which need reinforcing (as happens in a doublet) are not solid opal, nor are any pieces which have a non-opal backing, such as Mexican black basaltic opal matrix or boulder opal with a backing of ironstone.

The term 'true opal' is used to describe a fine play of colour which can be seen in the cut stone, no matter from what angle the face is being examined. It is a valuable property. The harlequin opal pattern, on account of its many-spangled colour play, gives a fine show of brilliant colours from all angles, an important feature of its value. Indeed the harlequin pattern is considered to be the most valuable of all opal patterns.

5 *The changing colours of opal*

The reason for the changing play of colour to be seen in noble and precious opal has been the subject of much conjecture. As long ago as 1845 Sir David Brewster, the Scottish physicist, said of opal, 'This gem is intersected in all directions with colourific planes, exhibiting the most brilliant colours of all kinds.

'The cause of these colours has never, we believe, been carefully studied. Mineralogists have said that they are the colours of thin plates of air occupying fissures or cracks in the stone, but this is a mere assumption, disproved by the fact that no such fissures have ever been found during the processes of cutting out, grinding, and polishing, which the opal undergoes in the hand of the lapidary. In submitting to a powerful microscope specimens of precious opal, and comparing the phenomena with those of hydrophanous opal, it is found that the colourific planes or patches consist of minute pores or vacuities arranged in parallel lines, and that various such planes are placed close to each other, so as to occupy a space with three dimensions.'

In 1862, another scientist, the Frenchman Descloiseaux, described opal in a similar way: 'Some varieties show an internal iridescent colour play of great beauty, which appears bound by the existence of very small interior cavities arranged in parallel rows in regular arrays, which give outstanding flamboyant reflections in good light.'

In 1871, a Professor Behrens made a deep inquiry into the nature of the colour play of opal and concluded that irisation in opal was due to thin curved lamellae, which had originally been formed as parallel plates, but were bent into curves, cracked, and broken up during the time of consolidation of the opal mass. Such lamellae, it was thought, must produce polarisation of light, and their very thinness must have originated colour. For the next ninety-three years, Behrens' ideas dominated gemmological thought on the nature of colour in precious opal.

However, the real breakthrough in understanding the origin of the colour play in opal came in 1964 when Australian scientist Dr J. Sanders made scanning electron photomicrographs of different opal varieties. He found that the difference between common and precious opal is in the basic structure of the opal material, and that a complete break in structural properties between opal forms exists. Opal is composed of minute particles of silica in closely packed spherical aggregates of uniform size which have a diameter ranging from 1500 Angstroms to 3500 Angstroms in discrete areas.

Subsequent work revealed that in gem-quality opal these silica microspheres are not only remarkably uniform in size, but also are packed together in very regular array. As they are spherical in shape there are tiny interstices or 'holes' remaining in the structure between them, and so these holes, too, are arranged in a regular three-dimensional array. Brewster's hypothesis of 1845 is now proved.

The presence of such an orderly array of minute cavities suggests that opal is an optical diffraction grating for visible light. The separations between the cavities are of just the right dimensions to cause light to be diffracted and, being arranged in a three-dimensional array, they cause various wavelengths in the diffracted light to reinforce one another at various angles. Incident white light is split into its full range of spectral colours: red, orange, yellow, green, blue, indigo and violet, and thus the colour play in precious opal is seen.

So much more of a technical nature can be said on the physical and chemical aspects of opal; however, we are equally concerned with conditions relative to the Coober Pedy opal region.

No matter the reason, be it for mining or tourism, it is important to know exactly what Coober Pedy has to offer the visitor.

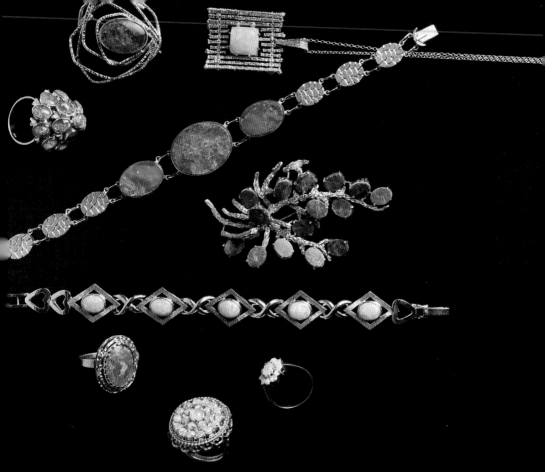

Opal solids, doublets and triplets fashioned into designer jewellery

Opalised seashell of high quality gem material mounted in gold. Shell found on the Sixteen Mile field

Piece of opal rough and a slice taken from it, cut and polished.

The Olympic Australis, considered to be the most valuable precious gem opal in the world. It was found in August 1956 at the Eight Mile field at Coober Pedy

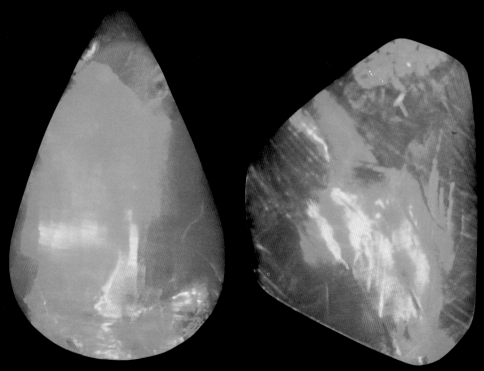

Left: Crystal opal shaped as a teardrop; right: Opal solid, harlequin pattern, from Coober Pedy

*Prized black opal, green
on blue, found at the
Mintabie opal fields*

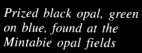

*Crystal opal solid from the
Mintabie fields*

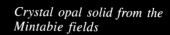

*Red fire opal, dark base, from
the Mintabie fields*

6 *Everything for the tourist*

In recent years Coober Pedy has developed into a tourist's paradise. No visit to the Far North of South Australia is complete if this fascinating opal town is not on the agenda; its world-wide fascination is attracting 20 per cent of all visitors to South Australia, with numbers increasing annually.

There is so much to see and hear that is unique to this area. Tours deep down into the opal mines and the dugout homes of the miners. Aboriginal handicrafts and opal-cutting demonstrations and other sights and events too numerous to mention. Coober Pedy's underground world is fascinating and the colourful community with its multicultural range of restaurants and clubs, fine motel accommodation and interesting shops has much to offer.

Parties holidaying can easily obtain mining rights to fossick for opal from the Coober Pedy Mines Department. They can visit the Breakaway, Australia's only lunar landscape, and the Painted Desert. They can visit the half-million gallon water desalination plant, go out to the famed Olympic field on the Eight Mile Digging and watch the miners at work.

Those wanting to come by road to Coober Pedy from Adelaide can do so in air conditioned comfort on the coaches. On arriving they have a choice of excellent accommodation at the Desert Cave Motel, the Opal Inn and other places, air conditioned bedrooms with private showers, hot and cold water, and liquor licences. The Desert Cave also has the luxury of a swimming pool.

Kendell operates a regular passenger service from Adelaide to Coober Pedy. Their comfortable aircraft passes over the St Vincent and Spencer Gulfs, numerous salt lakes and abeam the Woomera Rocket Range. Opal buyers from Adelaide use this service regularly.

Coober Pedy Tours will take visitors out to the fields to fossick and provide taxi hire cars and backpacker accommodation. They have an opal shop that provides a large range of inexpensive to valuable collector pieces of precious opal.

The South Australian Government Tourist Bureau has done a lot to promote Coober Pedy as a natural attraction; as well as being one of the state's richest assets, it is also a place where some of the most innovative commercial enterprises offer the visitor something different.

The Coober Pedy Miners Progress Association, Residents Association and the *Coober Pedy Times* constantly keep to the forefront not only the needs of the community but also those of the visitors to the town, wanting to provide the best of services while preserving that integral essence of the working outback opal town which brought tourists there in the first place.

Though the climate is severe with day temperatures high and nights cold, the tourists aren't discouraged. It is all part of the adventure.

7 *Conditions on the fields*

Since the first claim at Coober Pedy was pegged for the New Colorado Syndicate on 9 February 1915 and tracks were made into the vast out-back area there have developed hundreds of badly rutted roads going to as many different opal fields. An aerial view shows them as spider-webs snaking around thousands of shafts and conical mullock dumps.

The first recorded opal production, in 1916, was valued at £750, a lot of money in those days. Workings consisted mainly of trenches less than a metre deep along the edge of the escarpment. Opal floaters were plentiful on the surface and easily found in the shallow ground.

Early methods of mining were simple and inexpensive and there was opal galore, so much so it glutted a market that was unfamiliar with, and cautious of, the newfound gem. But conditions on the field were harsh and primitive. Very little water, heat and dust and the wind that then, as now, never seemed to stop blowing, lifting and dropping the sand in sheets, with visibility at times being nil.

It was 26 June 1920 before the Stuart Range Opal Fields Progress Committee, which had been formed in 1919 to provide a water supply, met to decide on a new name for the opal fields known then as the Stuart Range opal fields. Four names were suggested: Hutchison, Gemville, Opal Range and Coober Pedy. As we know, Coober Pedy was chosen.

In 1921 the Government installed a large underground water tank. The same year Hard Hill (Twenty Mile) was discovered, extending the then known potentially opal-bearing ground for a distance of 34 kilometres along the range. Available water encouraged more prospectors to Coober Pedy until 1940, when there were only 34 miners left on the field owing to opal production falling as sites were worked out.

In 1946 opal was found in shallow ground by an Aborigine at Geraghty Hill (Eight Mile), west of the present town. The discovery, together with the return of many miners and new chums from the Second World War and the establishment of new American markets, resulted in a spectacular increase in production. By the early 1950s, Geraghty Hill was considered worked out. However, in 1957 an Italian partnership sank shafts to 15 metres and discovered levels of precious opal below the old workings.

Due to the introduction of mechanised mining methods in the 1950s there has been continual expansion of the fields, reworked shafts and a concerted effort towards underground mining.

Today, the opal workings extend 30 kilometres north, 12 kilometres west and 8 kilometres south of the town's centre and are serviced by several major roads and hundreds of interconnecting dirt tracks.

With a floating population, there were 4500 people resident in Coober Pedy in 1989. The population fluctuates on a seasonal basis with short-term increases during holiday periods. Many miners and their families still leave the field during the summer due to the extreme heat and dust storms. Population fluctuation has decreased as bores north-east of the town provide a reliable water supply through a desalination plant. A town power supply enables air conditioners to be used in shops and homes, providing tolerable living conditions.

Established as the largest source of opal in the world, Coober Pedy is the major town in the Far North of South Australia, an important regional centre with school, hospital, community welfare, hotel/motel, shopping and commercial facilities second to none. It is the Outback with the sting taken out of it and tourism is an important industry well catered for, particularly since the sealing of the Stuart Highway. There is a sealed airstrip and regular air and bus services to Adelaide.

There are not as many sole prospectors fossicking on the fields or noodling on the dumps as there were ten years ago. There are many more blowers and bulldozers and drills searching out new opal territory with many large finds of precious opal being unearthed.

Conditions on the fields haven't really changed but many myths have been exploded. The old belief, for one, that opal stopped at a certain depth: now the poorer fields and those considered worked out are yielding gems of high quality with shafts sinking deeper and deeper.

The opal country is still dry bush-covered flats with saltbush predominating. There is very little timber except for mulga along the dry creek beds. There are low, sun-parched hills and in the Range itself there are innumerable rocky hills, eroded escarpments and dry water courses. On the tableland of the old eroded hills the surface is covered with gibbers, loose rounded stones resembling sunburnt porcelain.

The actual opal-bearing ground is very similar to other fields with a layer of desert sandstone resting upon a layer of opal dirt. This opal dirt is soft clayey rock.

The opal occurs in seams through the opal dirt and under a band or roof of sandstone and sometimes gypsum. It is also found as patches or pockets, or in veins of potch-and-colour with precious opal intermixed. Occasionally it is found as fossils—magnificent shells worth upwards of many thousands of dollars.

Coober Pedy opal is generally light in colour and is sold per ounce according to its brilliance. Most opal is sold in its rough state to the seasonal, resident and visiting Chinese buyers. Even the smallest opal chip has a value.

Looking out over the fields at the groups of blowers with their vent pipes saluting the sky, at the endless humps of mullock dumps and the noodlers crawling like flies over the dumps, there is a feeling the earth has been thoroughly plundered and there can be no more opal left to find. That is wrong. The knowing miners claim there is more opal still in the bowels of the ground than has so far come out of it.

Every time I return to Coober Pedy I go out to the fields to prospect and my efforts have never gone unrewarded. Down a shaft abandoned for many years I gouged $2600 worth of opal below a slide at the bottom of the main shaft. I could have gone down any of a number of shafts but I had what the miners call a gut feeling that there was opal down there, and I was right.

On my most recent trip I camped out on the Seventeen Mile. After spending a couple of days noodling the dumps for chippies I went picking in an open cut and found a rock 240 x 160 mm thick with a mass of 1100 grams. Back in Adelaide I cut and polished it and discovered I had a 300-carat stone of red-green fire opal worth a considerable amount of money. It had lain there waiting for me, missed by the bulldozer spotters.

Because there is no water on the fields it has to be carted and used sparingly. Plenty of water should be carried at *all times* and only short preliminary expeditions made until you have the feel of the land. That desiccating heat, that constant ball of fire, continually reminds you that this is arid desert country where most recently tourists have perished, their bodies recovered by the police.

Shortly after the 'piccaninny dawn' (the false light before the sun visibly rises) is the best time to set to work and finish before midday. If you are above ground you have done enough. If you are down below, comfortable, out of the blinding dust storms, then you can work for as long as you want. Your only annoyance, even underground, is the bush flies. There is no escaping them.

There is much to discourage the opal miner. Look out at the spinning dust on the horizon: a willy-willy. The skies darken as a blinding dust storm sweeps across the desert. The lazy, nagging buzz of the bush flies crawling into ears and mouth searching for moisture. The almost transparent 15 cm scorpions that climb into boots and sleeping bags and drop down shafts seemingly to wait for a miner to come down. The venomous snakes, the bindi-eye thorn creeper that tangles around feet and legs, and the millions and millions of gibbers rolling underfoot.

It's only worthwhile if you find opal.

These harsh conditions are only justified by the rapidly escalating price of precious opal. Its true worth is finally being realised and encouraging more would-be miners to go to the fields to make their fortunes.

There are two law enforcement bodies in Coober Pedy, the police and Mines Department officers. Both are there to keep the peace and to see that justice is done. The Mines Department has established rules which *must* be observed. If they are not, a miner can be ordered off the field, forfeiting anything that has been found and in extreme cases banned from coming back onto the opal fields. There are rules concerning how much ground a miner can stake and lay claim to. Mining rights have to be obtained before any prospecting can be carried out, available at the Coober Pedy Mines Department for a small fee. The Mines Department has a court to settle miners' disputes and they are a fount of up-to-date information. Without them chaos would reign.

In this updated edition of *Opals of the Never Never* I have called on and received tremendous assistance from the South Australian Department of Mines and Energy with the especial cooperation of Bruno Resignano, the information officer, who made slides and other material, invaluable to this work, available to me. The data from *Opal: South Australian Gemstone*, a Department of Mines handbook, includes descriptions of fields, location and growth of the fields as shown in the map on pages 6 and 7 of this book. To my knowledge there is no more comprehensive and up-to-date material available anywhere.

Over the years different names have been attributed to fields and inconsistent information given on dates and exact locations, making it very difficult to trace accurately the history and findings until S. Smart (a former inspector of Opal Fields) and other sources provided the summary below in chronological order, based on Departmental records.

1915-16 **Company.** Area of original discovery. Bulldozer cuts have obscured early workings.

Jewellers Shop and **Crowder's Gully.** Rich field, still worked in 1970-71. Now within town area and mining not permitted. Dugouts and roads have obscured most workings.

Big Flat. Extensive bulldozing has obliterated old workings below the scarp but some underground workings remain on the scarp. The field is now in the town area and contains some dugouts.

c.1918	**Saddle.** Older hand-dug workings bulldozed about 1970. Now in town area.
1920	**Jungle.** Now in town area.
1921	**Twenty Mile (Hard Hill).** Now forms western end of Vino field.
1930	**Ryan's Hill.** Deep hand-dug shafts on top of hill with extensive driving.
1946	**Geraghty Hill (Eight Mile).** First major discovery away from escarpment. Famous for the quality and abundance of opal. Underground workings on higher ground; bulldozer cuts in shallower ground to south and west. Several dugouts and shacks on field.
1946?	**Larkin's Folly (Nine Mile).** Thought to have been found about the same time as Geraghty Hill. Major activity in 1958 with some large finds and several periods of activity since. Underground workings and some bulldozer cuts.
1947?	**Allan Rise.** Most remote field, 44 km south-southeast of town near southern boundary of PSF. Two areas of workings, half a kilometre apart, consist of shallow bulldozer cuts and backhoe pits. Opal said to be in vertical seams and in poor levels in sand stone and in Russo beds. Erratic boulders (gilbey stones) and painted ladies are much more common than elsewhere in Coober Pedy.
1959	**South Pacific (Seven Mile).**
1963	**Greek Gully (Eleven Mile).** Large field, said to be a reliable producer of opal—a good 'tucker money' field. Consistently active.
1963?	**Zorba.** All underground workings. Surges of activity in 1984 and 1985, then intense activity extending field to east and south during 1986-89.Pre-1964 (exact dates unknown)
	Black Flag. Mostly bulldozer cuts with minor underground workings.
	Black Point. Now in town area.
	Crater. Small field on isolated mesa east of main scarp.
	Dead Man's Dugout. Partly in town area.
	Dead Man's Gully.
	Dora Gully (Twelve Mile). Started about 1948. Mainly bulldozer cuts.
	Emu Flat. Large field named because of the resemblance between miners bent over searching for floaters and a flock of emus. Extensive area of bulldozer cuts with underground

workings to the west.

Five Mile.

(Old) Four Mile. Several dugouts.

Fourteen Mile. Important field probably discovered early in the history of Coober Pedy. Major bulldozing began in 1968. Under ground workings are located on the higher ground, with a strip of unworked ground in centre of field. Consistently active.

German Gully. Now in town area.

Hans Peak (Nine Mile) (includes **Steinbiss** and **Stony Hill**). Large field with several areas of underground workings on top of scarp with bulldozer cuts and trenches below. Merges with Greek Gully to the northwest.

Lennon. Opal found initially in shallow ground, possibly in 1962. Extensive bulldozed area.

Potch Gully. Now in town area.

Russo's Folly (Ten Mile) (includes **Two Jays**). Underground workings on higher ground. Bulldozer cuts to the west.

Seventeen Mile. Large field which merges with Vino to the west and Fourteen Mile to the south. Underground workings and bulldozer cuts. **Shellpatch** (includes **Whiskey**). Underground workings and bulldozer cuts west of Stuart Highway. Backhoe trenches and bulldozer cuts east of Stuart Highway (Whiskey). Worked in 1954 and perhaps as early as 1923 with major activity during 1962-63.

Vino. Intensively bulldozed area on and below scarp west of Seventeen Mile. Also includes other workings around headwaters of Giddigiddinna Creek such as Hard Hill and Yellow Hill (listed separately).

Yellow Bullock. Several areas of hand dug shafts with shallow bulldozer cuts and backhoe pits near Yellow Bullock Waterhole.

Yellow Hill (Nineteen Mile). Named for unusual yellow-brown iron oxide coloration in Russo beds and top of sandstone.

Unnamed workings south of Yellow Bullock Bore. Two groups of scattered shallow workings half a kilometre apart.

*c.*1964 **East Pacific (Six Mile)** (includes **Jasper** and **Painters**). Extensive field. Mainly underground workings.

1964 **Perfetto.** Underground workings with many Yorke hoist dumps. Now partly within town area.

Olympic. One of the largest and most productive fields, with a reputation for good quality opal. Mostly underground working with some bulldozer cuts in older north central area. Consistently active field. In 1982-83 the field was extended westwards following discovery of Southern Cross.

1964-70   (exact dates unknown)

Turkey Ridge (includes **Butcher** and **Pitcher**). Scattered small areas of mostly shallow workings.

Brown's Folly.

Dingo. Shallow workings scattered along scarp southwest of Shellpatch with a second group 2 km due west of Shellpatch.

Hellenic Hill.

1964-70   **Willow.**

1969   **Kimba.**

1970   **Breakaways.** Very small field consisting of a group of backhoe pits 4.5 km southwest of the Breakaways lookout and a single bulldozer cut a kilometre to the southwest.

1971   **Avlis** (now part of Digger's Gully).

Hopeful Hills (includes **Watkins**). Now mainly a residential area with numerous dugouts along scarp. Watkins comprises a small area of workings at the northwestern end. Mostly now within town area apart from Watkins.

John Deere. Previously included in Seventeen Mile, this field was named in 1971. Numerous backhoe pits and bulldozer cuts.

Kenda Flat. Intensively bulldozed area along scarp with under ground workings up scarp to the southwest.

Mount Brady:

Opal Valley (northern) workings. Numerous shallow backhoe pits and bulldozer cuts around and below scarp with a few under ground workings on western margin. Some painted ladies have been reported.

Tee Valley (southern) workings. Scattered cuts and backhoe pits on scarp.

1972   **Deadhorse Gully.** Scattered bulldozer cuts and underground workings. Some hand-dug shafts pre-date 1972.

Piping Lane.

Prospect. Bulldozer cuts exposing shallow levels.

Unknown.

Wild Duck Plain (Long Creek).

1973   **Benito's Folly** (includes **Quail**). Several areas of bulldozer cuts. **Digger's Gully.** Intensive shallow workings adjacent to Stuart Highway. Most opal said to be alluvial.

	Jasper Gully.
1974	**Saturn.**
	Venus.
1975	**Frank's Folly.** Active in 1975 when named, but some workings present before 1970.
1976	**German Valley.** Now in town area.
1978	**Pluto.**
1980	**Mars.**
1982	**Southern Cross.** Underground workings concentrated in area of original discovery. Opal found at several levels. Groups of workings also a kilometre northwest and half a kilometre south of original area. Opal said to be patchy but of high quality.

1986

Halley's Comet. Very small field. Opal found by deepening of shaft first sunk by same driller many years before.

Jupiter. Originally one group of underground workings; recent activity on northeastern boundary adjacent to Zorba.

8 *Every modern amenity*

There is an air of excitement and luxury about Coober Pedy that is lacking on all other Australian opal fields. The miners have set about making themselves comfortable and have established homes for their families that rival and in some cases excel those in far-off suburbia. The children attend modern schools in town and are given the same education as children living in the cities.

After a hard day's work the family enjoy either private or communal swimming pools, eat and drink at the hotel or licensed restaurants, go to the drive-in, rent videos at the local store. No different from anywhere else except that they look out of their windows to the desert where they make their living.

Isolated, certainly, but with Adelaide only two hours away by air, it doesn't appear so threatening. And with the modern hospital and Royal Flying

The Coober Pedy Hospital, where every modern convenience is available

Doctor Service always at the ready, most emergencies can be easily coped with.

Because of their geographical location, the miners and their families are, by necessity, resourceful. Where else in the world does almost an entire population live underground in dugouts to escape the extreme heat and cold? With dugout shops and churches to pray in, all beneath the ground .

Many mining couples have learned the crafts of opal cutting and jewellery design and make their own exquisite and unique settings for the valuable gems they find.

Freight and mail are delivered by air as well as by road, so goods ordered by telephone today from Adelaide can arrive tomorrow. The nostalgia of camels bringing bare essentials to town has sadly gone and something has been lost in their passing, but that is part of the price of progress.

9 *Dugouts and troglodytes*

The miners living in the town of Coober Pedy have been likened to troglodytes because they live underground in specially-excavated caves called dugouts. Often these dwellings are spacious and contain four or five rooms. Living under the ground is an escape from the intolerable heat of the day and the icy cold of the night.

From the outside these dugouts resemble small hills with doors going into them. Inside, the rough rock walls often show the drill holes where gelignite or nitro-pill has been used during excavation.

Most families live in these unique underground homes. They are comfortably furnished and usually a small generator provides electricity. They account for the Aboriginal name for the town that means 'white man in a burrow'. Visitors to the town are so fascinated by these homes that miners invite them in; invariably they study the rock walls half expecting to see seams of opal.

Not only the homes are underground. Coober Pedy's Roman Catholic church is also a dugout and is said to be the only one of its kind in the world.

In 1975 a miner, Tony Pickering, purchased a dugout on the edge of town for twelve hundred dollars. He planned to bring his family to the field and saw the need to excavate an additional room. He worked in the evenings and weekends when he was not down his shaft on the Eight Mile. For a month he worked on the dugout when one night he uncovered a thin seam of opal in the wall. He started working in earnest and within hours gouged out a three-ounce parcel of precious opal worth about $1500.

Another miner sinking a septic toilet behind his dugout found a pocket of opal less than a metre below the ground and traces indicated a main lead running right under his home. He followed the lead and it ran into potch, but not before he had completely undermined his dugout (which caved in shortly after the seasonal heavy rains).

Some of the dugouts are large and lavishly furnished, incorporating pool rooms and swimming pools. One of them has been converted into a spacious art gallery.

It is only the Caucasians who live underground. The Aborigines prefer to live on top of the ground, being somewhat prone to claustrophobia. They will not go down into a shaft even if precious opal is there. They believe the only time people should go under the ground is after they are dead and their spirits have flown away. Because of this fear of going underground the leaders of the Aboriginal Community Council had to overcome considerable resistance when they proposed a takeover of the former Opal Inn Mine, which would give their people an opportunity to enter private enterprise.

10 *The Aborigines*

In 1976 leaders of Coober Pedy's Aboriginal community, the Umoona Community Council, bought the former Opal Inn Mine, a tourist attraction, and formed the Umoona Mine Co. In 1977 the company bought out one of its competitors, the Aladdin's Cave, for $50 000, and one of Umoona's directors, Mr G. Cooley, said the company in so doing had captured nearly half the Coober Pedy tourist trade. The Aboriginal community thus successfully entered private enterprise and the tourist industry.

This signified that at last the time had come when some of the wealth generated by the district's opal industry was to rub off on this land's original owners. It also meant that in visiting these Aboriginal-owned tourist attractions Caucasians were once again to become the guests of Coober Pedy's indigenous population.

When the newcomers first became 'guests' of Coober Pedy's nomadic tribespeople they certainly did not pay any fee for that privilege. Instead they pushed aside the Aborigines, dug shafts and plundered the area's treasure. Where the calloused feet of tribespeople had danced in corroboree since the Dreamtime the newcomers ravaged the land, rending it apart in their frantic search for riches. Only now, since the Department of Aboriginal Affairs has provided funds, has the Aboriginal community been able to make the purchases that have enabled it to share the profits of Coober Pedy's opal and tourist businesses.

Although progress has been made in the interests of the Aboriginal community, part of Coober Pedy's local colour is still that provided by the sight of nomadic Aborigines offering their bottles of opal chips for sale. These people and their families daily tramp the 24 kilometres to the outer opal fields to noodle the dumps and then return to town at night, thinking nothing of such a trek.

One cannot help speculating on the number of Aborigines in the past who were robbed of the products of their labour in the shafts or dumps of the opal fields. There is one story, among the many that are told, of an Aborigine who returned from his toil on the field to trade his finds to a local buyer. Among his stones were some exquisite gems and the buyer's eyes lit with greed as he regarded the brown-skinned man who stood before him. The buyer knew that where these stones had been found could lie a bonanza in opals. Why permit a 'simple black fellow' to reap such a harvest?

Only a guess can be made at the sum the trader paid the Aborigine for his stones. Obviously if anything like their trade value had been given the secret would have been out. Not only the Aborigine but the entire district would have known that a rich strike had been made. It is certain that the man who found the stones received but a fraction of their real value.

When the Aborigine made his way back to the site of his find he was not aware that he was being followed by the opal buyer. On arriving at the site his alarm can be imagined when a harsh voice from behind demanded to know what he was doing there. Before he could gather his wits the opal buyer launched into a tirade incorporating a recital of the penalties attached to jumping someone else's claim. The Aborigine stood awe-struck while the buyer pegged the area, declaring that it was his and that if the black man wished to avoid further trouble he would have to work the claim for him or face the consequences of his 'unlawful act'.

There isn't much doubt that this is just one instance of many where the Aborigines have been deprived of their rights on the opal fields and it is gratifying to know that now, through improved education and the good offices of the Department of Aboriginal Affairs, such exploitation has become a thing of the past. In their new-found freedom from white injustices and in their successful entry into private enterprise in Coober Pedy we can only wish the Aboriginal community continuing success in all their future efforts.

There is enough opal for all and around Coober Pedy the opal deposits are worth millions of dollars. It's hard work finding it but that's all part of the enjoyment for many holidaying prospectors.

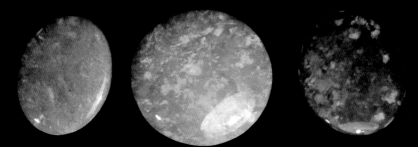

Solid black opal from Mintabie. Quality equal to similar gem material found at the Lightning Ridge opal fields

Below: Matching black opals cut from one piece of opal rough from Mintabie

Inset: Green on black, and pinfire opal from Mintabie

Red-green on black fiery opals from Mintabie

Crystal and white opal solids from Coober Pedy
Below: Seashell totally replaced with opal. Fine specimen from Coober Pedy

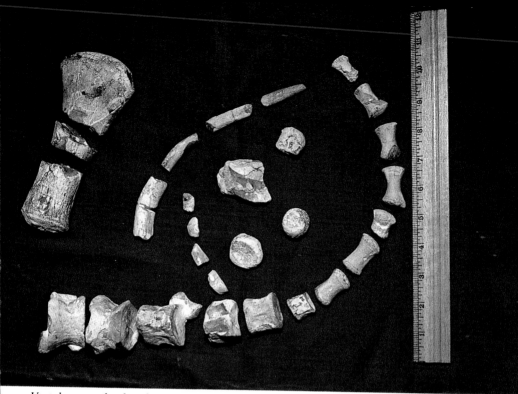

Vertebrae and other bones fully replaced with opal. Price beyond value.
Museum exhibit
Below: Clutch of opalised shells from Coober Pedy in original uncut condition

Acid-treated matrix opal from Andamooka

Gem quality opal doublet from Andamooka

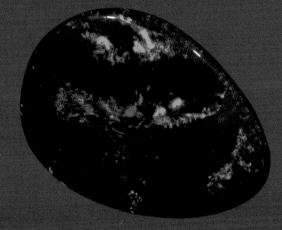

Gem quality crystal opal from Andamooka

11 *Let's go opal hunting*

It has been calculated by Barrie O'Leary, the opal mining consultant, that if all the opal in Australia could be mined and sold at today's prices, it would be worth $50 billion. This massive fortune is out there waiting to be won. Who knows how much of it is covered by just a thin veneer of clay easily removed by a prospector's pick?

What a fantastic family holiday is to be had hunting for opal—with sightseeing, adventure and riches to boot; the daydreaming, armchair study of maps, Mines Department reports and other available literature whetting the appetite as lists of tools, provisions and camping gear are drawn up. Soon what started in fun has become a serious business. Suddenly everyone knows all about opals and prospecting as fertile imaginations are fired.

We're going opal mining at Coober Pedy!

Annually the Coober Pedy opal fields attract thousands of tourists and holiday-makers from all over the world and they are all made to feel welcome by the locals. Everyone wants to get out and find their very own opal and the miners give all the help and advice needed.

The holidaying fossickers are not interested in sinking shafts or attempting open-cut mining. They arrive armed only with the essentials—only what they can carry: a pair of lightweight sieves, a geologist's pick and shovel, hammers, gads and crowbars. What they lack in hardware they certainly make up for in enthusiasm with their fervent determination to find opal. They have just as much chance as the veteran miner of striking it rich.

But the fossicker is faced with that problem common to all: where to look for opal. The countless mullock dumps beckon, but the prospect of sifting through even an average-sized dump is daunting, and time is at a premium. The abandoned shafts offer no hope at all for they dive 30 metres and more into the bowels of the earth, requiring extension ladders, ropes, winches and lighting.

The scientific approach, the detective that is inside all true prospectors, comes to the fore in a search to find host rocks and material that is common to opal. Opal gel is deposited in cracks and cavities or veins in volcanic and sedimentary rocks and it runs in veins through sandstone. Where there is a slide in the earth, a fall or a fault-line, there are great possibilities of finding an opal deposit. These 'faults' can be seen on the surface of the ground where outcrops of rock and sandstone appear like markers. Often floaters or bleached opal can be found around these rocky outcrops and traced back to a seam. When floaters are found it is certain that a lode is not too far away.

Opal can be a couple of centimetres or 30 metres under the ground while a seam can run for hundreds of metres, widening and narrowing as it snakes its course through the rocks and sandstone. It can dive down and run parallel then climb right back up and break the surface as an outcrop. There is no rule of thumb to say what direction opal runs and once a lead is found it has to be followed until it filters out. The lead could be common potch running into precious opal or visa versa. Potch is all too plentiful, but none-theless it can lead to a rich seam.

Coober Pedy opal is mined mainly from horizontal seams within a claystone that underlies sandstone. The opal can stop as suddenly as it started due to a fault line where the opal seam drops, perhaps 20 or 30 metres, creating what is called a new level. Fifty years ago the miners knew nothing of faults and simply abandoned their shafts, believing the opal had run out. Now many old shafts, taken deeper, are yielding beautiful opal that would have remained hidden without the help of geology.

Fossickers study the lie of the land taking in the run of the shafts and the outcrops. It is around these outcrops that they go to work needing only a pick and shovel and a sieve. The ground can be trenched to remove the overburden and to pick up a lead. A depth of half a metre is sufficient with width enough to shovel the trench out. The single purpose in trenching is to pick up a lead. It could be where opal gel is deposited. Not always is potch encountered, and even less often precious opal, but the host material is located and sieved through. Finding the smallest chip raises hopes and inspires frenzied digging.

So this is the lead the fossicker has been looking for and this is where opal will be found. Now the trench will turn into a small open-cut where a prospector's pick will gouge until it clinks on the glassy gel of potch or precious opal. There can be no mistaking the sound for the dull 'phut' of pick against clay.

The hit or miss method of mining can have its risks minimised by select-ing an area where precious opal has already been found. Some locations on the opal fields offering greater prospects than others include Shellpatch, the Fifteen, Sixteen, and Eighteen Mile fields, where tracts of virgin ground remain among the many shafts that have produced rich opal. The shafts in these locations are quite shallow and easily worked.

The Eighteen Mile and the Sixteen Mile Diggings pincer a low, flat-topped hill where many floaters of bleached opal have been found. Recently, hundreds of ounces of good jelly opal were found less than two metres under the ground around this location.

The Eighteen Mile Digging is worked by only a dozen miners who are taking the old abandoned shafts down from 12 to 25 metres where opal seams indicate a complex fault line. It is their belief that a rich bonanza of precious opal lies between the 25 and 30 metre levels.

There is so much unproven ground on the Eighteen Mile that if every miner descended on it it would take longer than a year before the entire area was explored. However, it's only a matter of time before another rich stone comparable to the *Olympic Australis* is found on this location for the ground gives every indication of containing precious opal.

It is almost always the lone prospector who unearths the most beautiful stones. The drivers of the massive bulldozers often miss whole seams of opal that are exposed then just as quickly buried by the scything blades of their machines. It is the gentle uncovering that reveals the bulk of precious opal, the turning of the dirt almost grain by grain; that has always been the way, and always will be.

Because fossickers are unhurried, their sharp eyes miss nothing. They slowly walk the open cuts after the bulldozers have gone and will, as likely as not, find a supreme gem buried under the merest skin of dirt.

Of all the fields it can be said that Shellpatch is the final frontier. Here a small community has been established in a natural gully. Children play and dogs scamper in a lazy, slow moving world far removed from city life and trauma. It is here the rich opalised shells prized in America and fetching extraordinary prices are found. With water bores and few mine shafts, Shellpatch could well be called the paradise of the opal fields, yet few tourists ever see it for it is too far from Coober Pedy, out beyond the more accessible fields, along a badly rutted track. Yet it is an ideal area, for here the fossicker with hammer and sieve will find plenty of alluvial opal.

12 *A woman on the fields*

Though there are a number of women living in the town of Coober Pedy there is not one living on any of the fields, so when a friend asked if I would take her along on one of my trips I refused point blank. I offered the usual, obvious excuses, closing the subject with the dictum that women did not belong on the field.

Shirley was forty, unattached and determined. She told me she would go to the diggings with or without me, so reluctantly I agreed to take her along but not without disclaiming any responsibility for whatever awful consequences might ensue. Women do not live on the fields or mine for opals unless they are in the company of men.

It was September and it was wet. It rained incessantly for twelve solid hours. The town of Coober Pedy was under water when we arrived and we barely managed to get in before they closed the main road. After that they kept it closed for ten days.

I was determined to get out on a field rather than be holed up in a motel so I took the flooded track that led to the Sixteen Mile Digging. We crept along at eight kilometres an hour, the Kombi perpetually diving into potholes where its wheels would spin uselessly in the mud. It took us five hours to reach the field and even then we would not have made it without the help of friendly Aborigines who shoved us through two very boggy patches.

A friend had given us the use of a tin shed for our accommodation on the field and we were very pleased to see it as we drove off the track and stopped the Kombi. We felt we could not have managed to drive another metre. We had finally arrived and here we would stay until the rain let up and we could get out to explore the field. Shirley's enthusiasm had taken a drenching but with true pioneer spirit she rallied and soon had a fire going in the hut so we could dry out. Nevertheless when I lit the kerosene lamps I did so with a feeling of foreboding. I was a fool. I should not have brought her here. This was a man's world.

In the morning the rain had let up and the sun was shining. We went outside to look around. In the mud were the paw-marks of dingoes and the toe-prints of emus which had come to investigate us during the night.

Our reconnaissance was suddenly interrupted by a cry of delight from Shirley. She had found her first chip of opal. It lay on the ground before her winking like a red fire ember. With our spirits somewhat restored we went around the mullock dumps and wandered completely absorbed through the open cuts. Fate had begun to smile on us. Within a few hours we had a handsome collection of opal chips.

As the days passed my fears of the consequences of taking a woman on the field began to evaporate. The miners drove by our hut calling hello and tooting their car horns and smiling at Shirley. Not one of them stepped out of line. Shirley had been accepted.

In the early evenings the miners dropped in for a chat and a cuppa. Shirley invariably had the billy boiling. They showed us their finds and invited us down their shafts for a look around. In no time Shirley had our visitors organised. They brought us groceries from town, posted letters and performed a hundred and one favours for us.

We made a strange friend, a Czech. His name was Velija. Several miners cautioned us that he was under suspicion of being a moonlighter (one who illegally enters and digs in another's mine at stealth). Unperturbed, Shirley invited him over for dinner one evening, telling him he would be most welcome at seven o'clock. He bobbed his head and with his little English said he would love to come.

Velija was an ox of a man: tall, with shoulders like a beer barrel. He had a shock of black curly hair and generally looked untidy but he had done a lot to help us settle in and make us comfortable.

On the night appointed for Velija's visit we had thick T-bone steaks brought from town at prohibitive prices. Shirley set the table and chilled a bottle of wine and we settled down to wait. We waited and waited. Seven o'clock passed and so did eight and nine and Shirley was beside herself. She declared the meal was ruined. Then came a timid tap on the door. I threw it open and in spite of myself started to smile. There was Velija with his hair plastered down with grease, beaming from ear to ear in his best suit. He clumped inside in a new pair of heavy boots and hung his head sheepishly.

We sat down in an awkward silence and ate without a word. The absence of conversation was intolerable. Shirley cleared away the dishes and I poured the wine, watching Velija fingering a strangling tie.

'Take it off and relax,' Shirley burst out, releasing the man from his torture. It was like watching a condemned person removing the rope. It also loosened his tongue and he started jabbering away. Finally Velija got up to leave and solemnly shook hands before going.

'Oh, look,' cried Shirley when he had gone. She picked up a small package left beside a plate and pulled it open. A beautiful polished opal rolled into her hand. It was Velija's way of saying 'Thank you.'

There were many interesting events on that trip but space prohibits recounting them all. The most exemplary was that a woman could find a place there, while being afforded every bit of respect expected and given to a woman in a city.

If more of the basic comforts were introduced to the fields undoubtedly many women would make their homes out there between the mullock dumps. A family could live much cheaper outside the town of Coober Pedy where living costs are sky high.

13 *Living costs*

Once upon a time opal prospecting was a poor person's business. Unfortunately that is no longer the case as most of the opal in shallow worked ground has been taken and deep mining requires expensive mechanised equipment. The pick and shovel are replaced by Calweld drills, blowers, bulldozers and tunnelling machines with great thirsts for fuel.

It used to be a poor person's hobby to visit the opal fields to set up home and live quite economically, having virtually no taxes to pay, no rent or rates or public utilities costs. Living was primitive but that was to be expected.

Nowadays it can cost upwards of $100 a week to rent a dugout in town. Electricity and desalinated water are available, at a price. Kerosene lamps and fridges are things of the past. There are council rates to cover the expenses of bitumen roads, public toilets and other amenities.

All foodstuffs have to be transported in. Rabbits and roos are no longer plentiful; T-bone steaks, beef, lamb and chicken are, at very high prices. The needs of a small family of three can cost another $100 a week. Add rent and food to basic mining equipment and fuel and you need a good income to afford to live in Coober Pedy.

How different from the days when a prospector came to the fields humping a bluey (a small pack containing all his belongings) and could pick up basic tucker at the general store 'on tick', because a man's word was his bond. Now everything is cash and carry and credit is out.

There is of course the alternative of going out on the fields with a tent or caravan or renting cheaply a tin shed and roughing it until you find opal and have a stake sufficient to be able to move into town. This still greatly appeals to some.

14 *Let's go touring*

Visitors spending a period of several days in Coober Pedy go on the very popular Perentie Outback Tour. Their host Peter Caust is also the proprietor of the Underground Bookshop in Coober Pedy. This fascinating trip to the Simpson and Painted Deserts, the magnificent Breakaways with superb views, is just the beginning of an adventure of a lifetime. Take the three-day trip to Oodnadatta and the Dalhousie Thermal Ponds, with dinner around a camp fire, the billy singing, and sleeping in a swag under the stars. Visit the historic Ghan railway ruins at Mount Dutton, Algebuckinga and Edward Creek on a round trip back to Coober Pedy over the Moon Plain Desert where a *Mad Max* movie was shot.

Peter is a professional photographer and your cook and guide with knowledge of the local flora and fauna, the best places to swim in the hot thermal ponds and the therapeutic mudpacks. He is a fount of information on birdwatching around the arid wetlands and where best to sight kangaroos, goannas, dingos, camels and donkeys. All food, utensils and swags are provided and vegetarians are catered for—even complimentary wines with the evening meals. Alternative trips to the outback of South Australia can be arranged with Peter.

Visitors on restricted timetables can go on the Coober Pedy–Oodnadatta Mail Run day tour, a 12-hour drive with the mail carrier visiting the remote outposts as the mail is delivered. Stops are regularly made to photograph flowing springs, remote townships, wildlife, ruins, cattle stations and the outback gibber landscapes. Again, bookings can be made through the Underground Bookshop.

The mail run starts at Coober Pedy. Passengers are picked up from the Last Resort Cafe by the Outback mail contractor on Monday and Thursday of every week in the year, excluding public holidays. This tour is on a more rigid timetable but much is crowded into the 12 hours, including a swim at waterholes or at the Pink Roadhouse with its in-ground 13 metre pool, and a journey past some of the sites of the Dreamtime. The vehicles are linked by high frequency radio transceiver into telephone networks, emergency services and the police, 24 hours a day. The vehicles are not luxurious but the drivers make sure the tour is as comfortable as possible. Vehicles are smoke free areas.

The route is on unsealed dirt roads graded every six months by the government and covers 600 kilometres of colourful terrain, dropping mail into the homesteads on the way. You may take your own food and drink or make purchases of a meal or light snack at Oodnadatta or William Creek. These major call points have liquor-licensed premises. The driver is an experienced operator and well known to the local people. He will stop for photographs, short walks, comfort stops and any point of interest as time allows.

There are other tours available but these two are outstanding.

Visitors with a yen to go it alone to discover the sights are discouraged from doing so. Not only is it easy to become lost in the Outback, there is the additional danger of countless deep mine shafts. The local police like to be advised so if you fail to return within a reasonable period of time, search parties can swing into operation.

15 *There's opal galore*

Nearly 75 years ago, 400 kilometres north-west of Coober Pedy, they found black opal in the hard ground at Mintabie. Initially the miners, iron men though they were, could not stand this hell hole with its long low ridges dwindling away into the infinity of the encompassing desert. They retraced their steps through Granite Downs and Welbourne Hill back to Coober Pedy with the news that there was 'opal galore' out there for any-one game enough to go after it, and black opal to boot. They showed their spoils to the miners but none of them would accept the challenge. They said there was enough opal around Coober Pedy without risking life and limb venturing further into the Never Never.

So Mintabie's magnificent black opal stayed in the ground until the prices for this rare stone soared and beckoned the new breed of miners with mecha-nised equipment and transportation suitable for reaching this far-off place.

It has been established by geologists that the entire region from Andamooka to Coober Pedy is one vast region of weathered Cretaceous rocks 70 million years old. It is possible that all the opal so far gathered in Coober Pedy is but a drop in the ocean compared to what is waiting to be discovered.

For many years Mintabie did not appear on any maps as it was too geographically and sociologically insignificant. That was before the million-dollar finds were made by small companies. Now everyone and their dog can tell you where Mintabie is and how to get to it.

In 1980 it was claimed that Mintabie's opal production could be in the $10 million a year bracket and mining equipment taken to the field was worth upwards of $7 million, including 30 bulldozers, mainly D9s, at a cost of $300 000 each. Activity decreased early in the 1980s, reached new heights from 1985 to 1988 and declined in 1989-91. Production over the past few years has remained stable with black opal from Mintabie currently supplying 40 per cent of world demand.

For the period 1934 to 1990, Mintabie opal production was, according to the estimated values by formula equated by the South Australian Depart-ment of Mines and Energy, $200 430 000. And for the period 1916 to 1990, $203 545 337. So much for the earlier estimation of the field's productivity being a mere $10 million a year.

Journalist Chris Butler describes it well: 'Mintabie is a fascinating place. Settled in hilly terrain, it has a natural beauty that is typical of the arid north of South Australia with sparse, low-level scrub and clusters of mulga. It has a harsh, unrelenting environment where summer temperatures regularly exceed 50°C and where, in winter, immense rains turn it into an impenetrable bog.'

An area of serious concern to the Government is the influence of mining on the Aboriginal settlement at Indulkana, some 40 kilometres away. The Pitjantjatjara Lands Right Act hangs over Mintabie like a dark cloud. It's claimed by the Aborigines that there are sacred sites in the area and that these are seriously threatened by continued mining.

However, 180 square kilometres of land around the present diggings have been proclaimed a registered gemfield and the Indulkana community is at present more concerned about the number of Aborigines going to the fields to noodle in the overburden.

The major problem confronting the miners at Mintabie is the rock, in parts up to 12 metres thick. It is very hard and has taken a toll of expensive equipment, holing bulldozer blades and wearing drills smooth. Another problem is the moist soil and low water table, making digging very hazardous.

The totally unpredictable runs of opal have confused many experts. A good run can stop abruptly and may be discovered on a different level some distance away. This has forced them to drill more holes and cut wider than in any other field.

It's said that Mintabie is undoubtedly the most difficult opal field to mine in Australia. But on the other side of the coin, Mintabie opal is a very good investment stone, extremely hard and superior to that found at Coober Pedy.

At present, 40 per cent of the total opal mined in South Australia comes from the Mintabie field. If it is expanded that figure could reach as high as two-thirds of total opal production.

From 1985 to 1989, in terms of value, the Mintabie opal field was the largest producer of precious opal, although the greatest volume still comes from Coober Pedy. The Mintabie workings extend for 8 kilometres along, and up to 2 kilometres west of a north-easterly scarp. In contrast to other opal fields, the area is well vegetated with mulga and mallee trees growing in a predominantly sandy soil. This reduces greatly the dust problems common to other fields.

An estimated 1000 people reside at Mintabie during the height of the mining season, but numbers decline markedly through the hot summer months with families returning to Adelaide, Coober Pedy and elsewhere. Living conditions at Mintabie are varied, ranging from the temporary and primitive to airconditioned brick or sandstone structures. The land is leased from the Department of Lands which in turn leases from the Anangu Pitjantjatjara Inc. Some camps are scattered through the mining area, the more permanent are located in the town area.

Progress has come to Mintabie in a rush since 1979. The Progress Association is very active and through fund raising has built a community hall and upgraded the airstrip, now one of the best all-weather strips in the Outback. A water tank and diesel pump provide water from a bore to the residents, and rainwater tanks have been installed at many houses. Telecom has installed two public phones and several private ones in the town area. With two licensed restaurants, a store, supermarket, school and a caravan park, the community is now well catered for.

It is important that visitors to the Mintabie fields obtain a precious stones field permit from the Department of Mines and Energy office at Mintabie, as this field is on Pitjantjatjara land and subject to the conditions set out in the 1981 Land Rights Act.

There are plenty of areas for the fossicker to noodle and the fiery black opal chips can be readily found and under more pleasant conditions than on other fields because of the lack of dust and winds.

There are excellent prospects for further finds of opal elsewhere on the Mintabie precious stones field. The Cretaceous sediments south of Old Field are most promising, as are the Mintabie beds in the west and south of the precious stones field, while the extensive outcrops outside the field indicate considerable potential to the west and south.

Indeed, there *is* opal galore and it is said that Mintabie may in time outstrip Coober Pedy both in value and production. Certainly the opal from this area is highly prized.

16 *The importance of knowing the fields*

While embracing Mintabie and Andamooka with Coober Pedy as one vast region containing opal, a further breakdown in localities must be considered, for Coober Pedy itself is not a single opal field. Coober Pedy is in fact nineteen small fields within a zone thirty-two kilometres long. These fields might well be called the suburbs of Coober Pedy and miners and fossickers should familiarise themselves with all of them before deciding to work in any specific area.

Not only should the geographical locations be known, it is a good idea to learn from the Coober Pedy Mines Department the yields and the types of material that have been found on these different fields because not all fields produce stable opal. The Seventeen Mile area has opal that is prone to crazing when brought to the surface and opal buyers view material from the Seventeen Mile with suspicion.

The Eight Mile, where the *Olympic Australis* was found, is constantly subjected to flooding as it sits on a water-table; because the top surface opal has been taken, mining in this area is at flood depth and pumps have to be used constantly and shafts timbered as the water makes the ground unsafe.

It cannot be said that any field around Coober Pedy has been totally worked out. There are several areas where it is extremely difficult to win opal and these are The Flats, Potch Gully, The Two Mile and Ryan's Hill. These are all in close proximity to the township and countless tourists with eagle eyes and great enthusiasm have swarmed over them.

Good fields worthy of looking over are The Follies, Zorba's, Farmers and Turkey Ridge. These locations are some 16 kilometres out along the Alice Springs road. All of these fields are being mined and a lot of precious opal is still being found.

Continuing along the Alice Springs road to the outer fields, numerous tracks lead off to different workings on the Ten Mile right out to Shellpatch. All of this is rich country.

There are many abandoned huts on the fields and a lot of opal is to be

Rear view of the Jeweller's Shop mine, an entire hill excavated with tunnels and shafts

found around them as chippies, where the miners have sat clipping their parcels, letting their snippings fall as unworthy to collect. But clippings from $500 an ounce for good opal is reliable tucker money when nothing better is offering.

It will take five hours to drive around all of the fields, allowing a little time on each for inspecting the ground. It will take months to become fully familiar with all the dry creek beds and markers around these fields but it is time well spent.

The Coober Pedy Mines Department, which is near the police station, is where reliable, sound information can be obtained. Other information and hearsay cannot always be relied upon. And a visit has to be made to this department to obtain a miner's right before any prospecting can be done on the fields. The Mines Department has a lot of helpful literature concerning claims and leases which should be obtained and studied. There are new laws concerning the use of explosives that should be investigated before going out on the fields and using gelignite at random.

In the centre of town is a general store and post office and in its foyer is a huge notice board that is of great interest with its offers of dugouts and huts to rent, machinery for sale, share-profit opportunities, local events, distress notices and information on arriving mail and parcels. It is equal to a local newspaper and the posting of advertisements is free. (The town itself is of great interest and is covered elsewhere in this book.)

Because the night closes in so quickly over the fields it is a good idea to time journeys on the way out to different areas so plenty of time can be allowed for returning. Strangely, at night, all tracks on the field look alike and shafts dive down at random. It isn't safe to travel in the dark along unfamiliar tracks. In fact it is easy to drive around in circles and miss the town of Coober Pedy altogether.

Many new chums have a fear of being lost on the fields which is quite understandable. In the event of becoming bushed it is essential not to leave the vehicle. It is easier to spot a car in the desert than a person on foot. If it is night then a fire should be lit a few metres away from the car. Don't leave headlights on to flatten the battery. During the day, in the heat, with water exhausted, remember the radiator. This reserve will often save lives. A solar still can easily be built by gathering vegetation and putting it over a container in a scooped hole covered by a plastic sheet with a pebble in its centre. The sun will draw up the moisture from the vegetation and condense on the plastic sheet to drip back down into the container. Enough fluid can be gathered this way for survival. Above all, don't panic—eventually someone will come along and find you.

In going exploring it is wise to tell someone the direction you are taking and the estimated time of your return. The police station will be happy to accept this information and make a point of watching out for you. That is part of their job.

The matter of survival in Coober Pedy is not as acute as it was several years ago. There are so many miners and fossickers active on the fields that help, when it is needed, is usually close at hand.

17 *The fossicker*

The opal fields of Coober Pedy are ideal for the fossicker who wants to rummage about without getting involved in actual mining for opal. A minimum of equipment is needed, in fact a geologist's hammer, a pair of tile snippers, a pair of sieves and a dilly bag are all that is really required.

Unlike other gems, where stone identification knowledge is important, opal clearly identifies itself with its colour and established hardness. On other gemfields associated stones are found: for example, spinel and garnet are always found in the locality of sapphire. Opal has no close relatives other than potch.

Fossickers therefore are of single purpose when they come to the opal fields. They know what they are after and cannot find a second best for there is only opal. Footloose and unhindered by heavy mining equipment the fossicker can roam all over the Coober Pedy opal fields in search of alluvial opal at outcrops, on mullock dumps and in the wash of the dry creeks and river beds.

Fossickers seeking specimens for their collections will not be disappointed. Within a few days a weighty load of potch and colour, chippies and a few solids will be your reward if you spend time going over the ground where opal has been already found.

The miners encourage the lone prospector and fossicker and readily invite them to visit their shafts. They will allow their mullock dumps to be noodled and often permit fine veins of low grade opal to be gouged under-ground by the fossicker. They will pass on their knowledge and point out good areas for fossils where opalised shells and belemnites have been found. Above all they'll yarn about opal if they have the time. They'll tell tall tales of the opal they nearly won and the opal they're going to get, eventually.

The only people who can come to the fields and move around at will, in the manner of the early miners, are the fossickers, for they are carefree and uninvolved. They can move through the nineteen fields that make up Coober Pedy, stopping a while here, a little longer there and then moving on. Their camp fires traditionally burn on the field like a beacon and in the firelight the day's find will be inspected and tomorrow's general direction planned.

Elevated view of Coober Pedy town centre
Below: High-rise Desert Cave motel, much of which is also underground,
setting the style in the desert oasis of Coober Pedy

The Catacombs church in the centre of Coober Pedy township, used by all Christian denominations
Below: The Catholic church, entrance and belltower

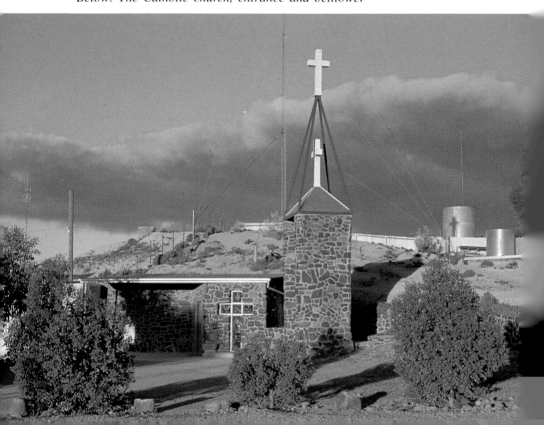

The home of the colourful artist Crocodile Harry (inset), a living legend in
the outback, is visited by tourists from all over the world
Below: Thursday at the Miners Store in Coober Pedy

Facade of this dugout is deceptive—it goes down into the bowels of the earth
Below: Every comfort in a home beneath the ground

There will always be fossickers for it is inherent in humanity's makeup to probe, gouge, inspect and collect, and in their own way the fossickers make new discoveries and open up fresh territories. No matter where they go on the gem fields, fossickers are always made welcome and invited to share what the field has to offer.

The miners do not regard fossickers as competition, seeing them as akin to the scientist, observing, collecting small amounts of stone, studying the formation of the ground, awed at what nature has provided. Fossickers are casual, easy-going and placid. If they didn't have this nature they wouldn't be fossickers.

The world of geology is the fossicker's oyster. Without greed, fossickers select specimens for the pleasure they give rather than for their monetary value. Perhaps it is because of this that Dame Fortune smiles on them more often than on others. Fossickers have a knack of finding the most beautiful stones, often quite by accident.

Fossickers around Coober Pedy need only a miner's right to search for opal. This permit provides the holder with many benefits and privileges legally arranged by the Mines Department and too numerous to mention in this book, but the Mines Department has literature concerning the entitlements. Without a miner's right a department official can confiscate everything that has been found and order an offender off the field.

18 *The prospector*

There is a great deal of difference between a fossicker and a prospector. Fossickers rummage about often with neither too much direction nor foresight, hoping they might by chance find what they are searching for. Prospectors have a wider view and a reasonable hope of finding what they are looking for based on a scientific study of their subject matter.

The prospector who goes to the Coober Pedy opal fields will most likely mingle with the miners to benefit by their experiences before going out to survey the land.

The prospector's kit, by necessity, will be more extensive than the fossicker's. Prospectors also need a miner's right from the Mines Department before going onto the fields to prospect. As well, a geologist's pick and sieves, shovels for trenching the ground and a heavy and medium-weight pick are required.

Working in the same manner as a geologist, prospectors collect samples of excavated dirt and make notes concerning the strata of the ground. All this is preparatory to mining at a later date. They examine the field, the extent of leads, the levels where opal dirt is encountered, referring to Mines Department records constantly. They have sets of maps, topographical and geographical; and information on the faults and folds of the ground and its history of volcanic, glacial or thermal upheaval. They understand the formation and settling of opal gel, the cause of its changing colours, its hardness, composition, fracture and specific gravity. In their own way they are professionals and may have visited other opal fields to study their deposits.

In the final analysis prospectors rely only on their own judgments and rarely confide their findings to anyone unless employed to do so. Like the fossicker, the prospector is a loner. The miners are generally wary of prospectors for they are both after the same rich deposits.

Only when completely satisfied that there is a strong possibility of opal being in a determined place will the prospector take out a mining lease and peg a claim. Strangely, most miners do not prospect to the same extent and are satisfied to start mining immediately after finding a hopeful lead.

Prospectors are unhurried. They might sink a diamond drill in several places to different depths before finally putting down the shaft. Beforehand they will analyse the material found in the diamond drill cores, making copious notes that will assist in putting the hole down. Step by step as they sink the shaft they know what to expect: how thick the grey billy and jasper is and exactly where the opal dirt rests.

Large mining companies searching for gold, wolfram, tin, copper, nickel or gem stones will rely on a prospector's report and they employ prospectors to go out to do field research. There is nothing haphazard about their operations—there cannot afford to be with shareholders' money at stake. They have to be positive that what they are after is in fact at a predetermined depth. On this information they base their estimates of mining costs.

The average miner is a dyed-in-the-wool gambler and sometimes hasty to get on with the job. Miners have little time for scientific appraisals but they respect the prospectors and to some extent understand what they are doing. But it isn't for them.

The miner is after the big rich parcel beneath the ground and is not interested in the surface chippies and small stones. Miners will not spend time noodling on the dumps unless they are desperately short of money, when noodling becomes a last resort. The prospector will noodle because the dirt on the mullock dumps indicates what can be expected underground. And the chippies and stones they find help to cover expenses.

19 *Noodling for opal*

Noodling over mullock dumps and through the open cuts is a highly profitable form of fossicking. The practice of sifting through discarded opal dirt can yield beautiful opals.

Working the dumps in search of opal

Some miners, discouraged by sinking unprofitable shafts, have become professional noodlers, building elaborate noodling machines ranging from 'puddlers' to conveyor belts.

These belts, usually driven by petrol motors, travel through a lightproof shed where a battery of ultra-violet lamps show up opal as pale blue blobs. Unfortunately scorpions emptied onto the belt with the opal dirt also show up as pale blue blobs and viciously sting the noodler picking them up as opal. Outside the tin shed a front-end loader transfers a mullock dump to the moving conveyor belt in a matter of hours. Inside the lightproof hut the noodlers sweat profusely as they stand beside the belt watching for the pale blue blobs.

Some professional noodlers earn as much as a thousand dollars a week.

The noodlers swarm over the dumps armed with sieves of all shapes and sizes, scooping the dirt up into them and furiously shaking them, scattering the peppery dust to the wind. It blows into their eyes and mouths but it doesn't seem to worry them. Carefully they pick out splinters of opal from the sieves and pop them into bottles and matchboxes. Within a few hours they have burrowed deep into the dump.

Opal is not only found on the dumps. Large pieces have been found in the massive open cuts, deep furrows sometimes a hundred metres deep and just as wide. The bulldozer pushes the dirt before it with a scooped blade while behind the machine a ripping blade lays open the opal level.

Along the dry creek beds the fossickers look for 'floaters': weathered pebbles of opal washed from an outcrop. These often look no different to the surrounding gibbers and need to be snipped to see if they have any colour. When there is colour the stone is probably crazed from being out in the sun and is only worth breaking up to put in with chips.

The eager tourists who haven't the time to put down a shaft troop through the open cuts with their heads bowed and let out frenzied cries when they find a gleaming chip of opal.

It really is here, on the ground, waiting to be picked up!

20 *Puddling, rumbling and sieving*

Quite apart from shaft and open-cut mining is the sieving and rumbling for opal; where there is a scarcity of water, dry puddlers are used. These are inexpensive machines which extract opal from kaolin clays, schists and sandstones.

Basically a puddler is a large motor-driven drum lined with 50 and 25 centimetre mesh. Opal dirt is shovelled into the drum as it slowly rotates to filter through the screenings, leaving only rocks, potch and opal to be eventually hand-sorted. Protruding from the drum is a funnel that disgorges the waste dirt onto a dump. Often a puddler is utilised alongside a shaft hoist that draws up the dirt from underground, thus saving the miner working below from hand-sorting. A single person operating a puddler can process as much as five tonnes of dirt a day and almost no opal is lost in the process.

Rumblers work on virtually the same principle as tumblers, inasmuch as the mesh separation system is utilised. The rumbler is a wire mesh bed fastened to a sturdy frame that vibrates through a belt/motor operation. A pulsator attached to the motor trembles the fine dirt through the wire mesh. Again the opal is hand-picked and the waste disposed of. The rumbler (more common on the Lightning Ridge field) is excellent for sorting through old mullock dumps.

Belonging in the range of mesh separators is of course the humble and much used hand sieve which has so many uses above and below the ground. The most useful sieves are the duals: two sieves that lock one inside the other. The diameter may range from 0. 4 to 1 metre with depths varying from 6 centimetres to a metre.

The operation of a sieve is quite simple. The dirt is scooped or shovelled into the top sieve which is agitated to filter the finer material through while retaining the larger material. In some cases these sieves may be suspended from tripods. Hung at a convenient height dirt may be shovelled into them. A wire is fastened to the sieve and tugged to agitate the sieves to sift the dirt through. The suspended sieve allows the operator to have both hands free to clear a mullock dump.

Puddlers and rumblers can be built on the field with a minimum of expense, the main purchase being the motor. There are puddlers motorised by the back wheels of vehicles. A drive belt is fitted around the hub to drive the puddler shaft. The advantages of this mechanisation are speed regulation through the car gears, and the convenience and cheapness of petrol operation.

Along with puddlers, rumblers and sieves are the dry sluice boxes that can be used almost anywhere on the fields. These long troughs of wood or tin are suspended by wire at a 45° angle. A fine mesh trunk is fitted to the sluice at the end nearest the ground. The dirt is shovelled into the box and gravitates down and through the fine mesh leaving the opal and large waste to be hand-sorted.

Any device that can separate the fine dirt from the bulk material is acceptable. Even wire bed mattresses have been put to use as gigantic sieves.

By necessity miners are an inventive breed. They have fitted meshes over the emptying mouths of blowers that suck the opal dirt from under-ground like huge vacuum cleaners. The only disadvantage to this is that someone must be constantly on hand to clear the meshes so they do not become back-blocked with the great volume of dirt sucked up through the tube. Opal dirt is shovelled and separated in concrete mixers, washing machines, spin dryers, anything that will rotate and disgorge fine dirt.

These methods of hand mining are not new. Right at the beginning miners realised the importance of dirt separation and were the first to devise sluices and dirt races, some operated by running water on the edges of streams and rivers where there was an abundance of alluvial material. Mainly the wet sluices were (and still are) used for gold catching.

The simple use of a few sheets of old tin and mesh can save countless hours of hand noodling over dumps. These materials are inexpensive and light to carry, easily erected and very practical. Inventiveness is a key word in mining. Initiative and using the best means available to find opal often saves time and heavy labour. If one is to be a miner then one will of course need some basic mining equipment.

21 *The miner's equipment*

When the opal fields were first discovered everything needed there was transported by drays or even on handcarts carrying only the bare essentials; for this reason equipment was quite primitive for many years. Shafts were sunk with pick and shovel and the mullock (unwanted rock) was hauled from a hole by a hand windlass. This simple device is still used by some of the old timers and those who cannot afford up to date machines. Most windlasses are now powered by compressed air or petrol-driven engines.

One of the most useful machines is the Yorke hoist, a petrol-driven winch operating a swivel head mounted to a derrick. The dirt is hoisted to the top of the hole and a top man can swing it clear to pile a mullock heap away from the shaft. An improvement on this is a self-unloader, an automatic bucket tipper that can be operated by a miner underground. The bucket is drawn to the surface by a winder motor along two parallel curved rails a few metres above the shaft, with rail extensions to clear the hole so the dirt can be tipped. At the point of tipping a reverse switch is automatically operated to return the bucket along the rails and back underground.

More than ever now, miners work in teams called 'companies' that enable them to pool their financial and labour forces and utilise machinery adapted essentially for opal mining, such as blowers, gigantic vacuum-cleaners mounted on flat-bed trucks; bucket elevators, continuous chains fitted with scoops to raise the mullock to the top; and tunnelling machines, augers taken underground in pieces and reassembled to cut drives like huge corkscrews which spew the dirt onto conveyor belts or feed it to blowers to be carried to the top of the shafts.

Mechanised methods are employed to take much of the risk out of hit or miss shaft sinking with exploratory drilling by Calweld drills. The auger drill is a larger investigator rig that can burrow down over 20 metres. If opal chips are brought up in the cores it is considered worthwhile to start sinking a shaft.

Undoubtedly the most expensive form of mining is open-cutting, which is adopted when opal is relatively close to the surface or in pockets rather than levels. Massive bulldozers rip and push away the overburden, then spotters walk behind the machine as it cuts swathes, driving back and forth and moving layers of ground to reveal the opal pockets and seams. As soon as opal is found the bulldozer moves out of the cut and it is up to the eagle-eyed spotters to use hand tools, cleaning down to below the opal level or to opal-bearing dirt.

Many a time a tourist or prospector has walked through an abandoned opal cut and found precious opal that has been missed by the spotters. A thin veneer of dirt can hide a pocket of opal worth many thousands of dollars.

Because precious opal can be locked in conglomerate and clays, noodling machines are now used to reharvest the mullock dumps. A front-end loader lifts and drops the mullock into a raised hopper, a trommel screens out the fine material and the rest is fed onto a conveyor belt that travels through a specially-erected shed that has no windows or ordinary internal lighting. The darkness is lit by ultra-violet light. Opal, potch (and scorpions) fluoresce in the ultra-violet light, enabling hand-sorters in the shed to gather them from the continuous conveyor belt that carries the waste through and out to form a 'dead' mullock heap. One of the risks involved is picking up a scorpion from the conveyor belt and being bitten; though not fatal, the bite does make you very sick.

When a very large open cut is undertaken scrapers are used to excavate and shift overburden ripped by the bulldozer. Up to a dozen people can be employed in a company putting in big opal cuts at a cost of thousands of dollars with, often, very little patchy opal being found. A lot of the money earned from opal goes back into the ground in the endless search for more.

Modern-day methods have come a long way from the times when miner's picks, noodling sieves, shovels and gads were the basic essentials. Ladders were handmade then, as were the hand windlasses. Lighting was by candles and kerosene lamps. Now it is compressors and generators. Soft cloth hats and fly nets have been replaced with hard hats and goggles. Cloth dillybags made of calico for carrying rock specimens, made the same as the drawstring marble bags that children use, have been exchanged for geologists' cases. Gone are the drays and handcarts as four-wheel-drives hurtle through the opal fields. Portable homes stand where tents and caravans housed the mining family. Coober Pedy has entered the high tech age but otherwise nothing has changed—the flies, the dust, the search for the elusive opal.

Nonetheless there is still a place for humble prospectors carrying swag, tent, miner's pick and shovel, with dilly bag swinging from their belts as they search for a site, virgin ground to sink the pick in, perhaps to clink on potch or a pocket of beautiful flashing, fiery opal.

Requisites for the hand miner are basic: a good rucksack will hold most items and fit comfortably across the shoulders during expeditions. Depending on circumstances a two-person tent can be handy, with a strong groundsheet, and a sleeping bag and small stove. Sleeping under the Coober Pedy stars is most pleasant. And cooking on an open fire is part of the adventure of being on the fields.

There is absolutely nothing to be gained by being burdened down with every tool and device that might be useful. Obviously things such as matches, candles, first-aid kits and water bottles are a must for both prospector and fossicker. Tools can be stored wherever you set up camp rather than trudging around carrying them wherever you go. The novelty of searching for opal soon wears off, plodding on foot, laden up, looking for that special spot to dig.

It may take you days, time permitting, to choose your site, and when you find it you'll want to be fresh and enthusiastic, ready to get to work.

22 *Choosing your site*

There is one question that can never be accurately answered. Where is the best place to find opal? Every miner has scratched his head when he has had to choose a new site.

It's simple really because opal is where opal was. That is to say, where opal has been found there is likely to be more.

There are Aborigines who claim they can smell out opal and other people argue that a divining rod can be used. But there is another way and it is one that has the most chance of being successful. A sturdy pick and the ability to sweat gallons of brine and a heart as big as a house—the employment of all these things aided by a lurid vocabulary will win precious opal.

On the fields there can be five hundred metres of ground and one lone miner. If that miner shouts 'OPAL', within an hour that ground will be as busy as the Melbourne Railway Station at peak hour. Then the blowers move in after the diamond drills and the shafts dive down. A new site has been started.

The ground tells a story. It slides and runs in levels and a good miner can read that ground. The ability to recognise 'probable' ground comes with experience.

Common to opal fields are flat-capped hills like weather-beaten mounds of desert sandstone with the tops sliced off. The sandstone of these hills rests on opal dirt and once that is found the quest begins.

An entire hill does not have to be excavated to uncover a seam of opal dirt. This dirt is called the 'bottom' and exploring a hill, picking away as you ascend, will often establish where this 'bottom' is. Bottom in opal terminology does not mean the base. The bottom could be halfway up or right on top of the hill, covered with a layer of grey billy (hard silicified claystone). It could shear right out of the ground as an outcrop with its precious opal bleached and crazed by the sun.

In searching out opal dirt it is advisable to look around for floaters, bleached pieces of potch or weathered opal outcrops. The potch and opal floaters then have to be traced back to their source.

But following a trace of potch isn't as easy as it sounds in gibber country

A successful one-man show. Mining the old way, this miner struck a patch of opalised shells, a great result

where one weathered stone looks pretty much like another. The traces of potch could have come from a level of dirt hundreds of metres away during the erosion of a hill. If a trail of potch seems to lead nowhere then chipping at an exposed face on a nearby hill could provide further leads.

Finding bottom in the side of a hill naturally makes mining easier as a shaft does not have to be sunk and dirt does not have to be hauled to the surface. A tunnel is driven into the side of the hill following the opal dirt which generally lies under a layer of sandstone, and this sandstone makes an excellent roof to work under as it is stable.

Opal prospecting is literally fossicking at the grass roots level for often an outcrop of potch and colour spears right out of the ground. Years ago when surface opal was plentiful it was picked up off the ground by stockmen as stones broken by horses' hoofs, ablaze with fiery reds—brilliant opal.

So when opal dirt is located and it contains a seam of potch and colour, the site is found, and it is there that a level has to be followed or a shaft put down. The level might not 'make', it could be a duffer, a squibby level. That does not mean the site has to be abandoned. The shaft should be taken deeper to the next level, and if necessary to the next. Who can say exactly where the true, opal bearing level is?

Many a miner has won rich pockets of opal by taking an abandoned shaft down to a further level. This was the case on the Eight Mile field where the fabulous *Olympic Australis* was found in 1956. An abandoned shaft, a squibby level that yielded very little opal, with the real bonanza just five metres deeper—and worth a fortune.

23 *Sinking the shaft*

There is one sure, proven way to find opal and that is to sink shafts. Obviously there is much more opal beneath the ground than there is on top of it. The more shafts sunk, the better your chance of locating opal.

In putting down a shaft several aspects have to be taken into consideration. The length and width, even the shape of the hole is determined by the miner. Whether you are large or small. Can you work in a confined space or do you need room?

Basically the sides of the shaft are cut square like a trench but they will not stay that way for long because invariably a square hole ends up with its sides hollowed out and so becomes round.

After the overburden (the top layer of leaves and dirt) is cleared away and the hard virgin ground exposed it is time to start swinging the pick.

A Calweld drill sinking an exploratory shaft on the Zorba field

Steady picking at the ground will result in better progress than fierce sledge-hammer swipes that ultimately must result in exhaustion. The pick is swung mechanically until the ground is broken up and can be shovelled onto a mullock dump. You've made your mark and now you are making your own dump.

How deep you will need to go is decided by the depth of the opal level. If it is found at less than three metres then a windlass will not be needed for the dirt can be thrown clear of the shaft with the shovel, but any deeper means the dirt has to be sent up the shaft in a bucket.

As the shaft deepens it is advisable to line the head to prevent the evacuated dirt and rocks falling back down from around the mouth. The lining can be done with old sheets of tin, corrugated iron or logs if they are available. This heightens the shaft mouth above the dump, forming the sides of the mullock dump that will surround it.

Most shafts require a windlass or a Yorke hoist (a mechanical, motor-driven winch); these can be bought in Coober Pedy or from miners leaving the field. Until a few years ago they had to be constructed on the site and a miner had to search for kilometres to find raw material—a suitable log to make a windlass barrel.

Professional miners prefer to work in pairs; they form a company by mutual agreement, on a handshake, sharing the work, the losses and the profits, if any. One miner works below, hacking at the ground, filling the buckets, drilling and detonating the gelignite or nitro-pill. The top miner winds up the dirt, empties it, sends down tools and explosives and spreads the dirt as the mullock dump grows. Down the shaft is the miner picking, shovelling, driving a shaft, day after day after day. It could take up to three months to bottom. Hopefully the shaft will bottom on potch and colour. It's only a dream that it could actually bottom on precious opal. It does happen, but very rarely.

At last the pick rings on the last iron band. Penetrating the band the miner is now onto the layer of opal dirt and faced with the moment of truth. Is the shaft a duffer? Ninety-five out of a hundred are. The shaft has bottomed, but is it on potch and colour, precious opal or nothing?

The shaft could be six to ten metres deep. Maybe the opal dirt is a squibby level! Is it worth driving deeper to the next level and the next? Alternatively another shaft has to be dug. . . A level has been reached and there is potch and colour. Now a drive is put in to follow it. The trace may be a razor-thin seam of opal.

The lighter pick is used to gouge away the soft sandstone and kopi and progress is slow. Sometimes only a metre of ground a day is covered, for great care must be taken. It isn't hard to miss a small pocket of opal.

Bucket elevator at work on the Olympic field

Chip-chip-chipping away, gouging out the glassy potch by the light of a flickering candle. On hands and knees in deathly silence. Kicking back the loose toe dirt with both hands locked around the short handled pick.

'Crack!' The pick grazes a pebble of glass. But there's no glass down here! The pick scrapes away as gently as a surgeon's scalpel, a sliver at a time. Suddenly, a flash of vivid orange lit up by the spluttering candle and a sparkle of green. It is there!

Down in the utter quiet of the underground world there appears a flame of life: the fire of precious opal.

It might only make in a small patch and run out. It is gouged carefully and inspected as it slips into the palm of the miner's hand, then it is dropped into a cotton dilly-bag hanging on a belt.

Time stands still. There could be an Aladdin's cave of rich opal only centimetres away . . .

The luxurious Opal Cave. A veritable treasure trove offering visitors the finest gem quality opal at field prices
Below: The Underground Bookshop owned by Peter Caust, a professional photographer who supplied many of the fine pictures used in this book

The Old Timers' mine, a honeycomb of drives where precious opal was found
Below: Opal gougers at work underground

Sunset over the Five Mile extension
Below: The last light of dusk on the north-west ridge

North-east view of the Breakaways outside Coober Pedy
Below: Hospital Hill dugouts, Coober Pedy

24 *Mechanised mining*

Veteran opal miners on the fields simply are not interested in noodling the dumps for chippies or 'tucker money'. They are after the rich seams of precious opal and the name-stones, and often have invested hundreds of thousands of dollars in mining machinery. They think only of the big strike, the million dollar find and that is their goal.

Professional mining calls for diamond drills, blowers and huge bull-dozers. These miners use dozens of cases of explosives a week and drums of diesel oil. They operate underground tunnelling machines that look like gigantic corkscrews, boring into the walls of the shafts making drives, the dirt carried away along railway lines on big steel trolleys and taken to the surface by mechanical escalators.

Professional miners think big and work hard, often twelve and fourteen hours a day. They must because of their capital investments in the big risk enterprise that opal mining is.

No matter the cumbersome, technical machinery, miners have first to find a lead in much the same way as the humble fossicker before they can set their machinery in action. When they do find a lead they employ a drill to establish the depth of levels the opal runs through. This crane-like derrick mounted on a flat-bed truck spins a diamond-tipped hollow drill into the earth. The hollow drill collects a rock-sample core as it worms its way down and the miner inspects this core for traces. A trace can be conglomerate or potch or, with a great deal of luck, opal.

If the diamond drill establishes there is opal below then the miner opens up the shaft to the indicated depth and installs a hoist that is driven by petrol or diesel or steam. The hoist lowers a drum which will remove the mullock. A lighting plant is installed, working off a small generator the size of a motor bike engine. This not only provides electricity for lighting but also powers drills that will bore the holes for explosives. All this work and expense can take up to a month with no financial return to the miner. And the search is not over yet.

Shaft ventilation is vitally important. A blower has to be brought to the top of the shaft and long snaking aluminium pipes taken down to the level and into any drives that are running from the shaft. This huge vacuum cleaner will suck out the deadly fumes left after explosives blasts and the clouds of dust from the shattered rocks and sandstone.

Now the miner is ready to go to work to find the elusive opal.

Down the shaft and on the level where the diamond drill cores indicate a lead the miner picks away with a geologist's hammer—a detective searching for a clue. Brown iron-stain markings in a layer of white clay may be found or the hammer might strike the welcome 'clink' of potch. Moving around with a lamp, inspecting the walls the miner marks with a pick places where holes must be drilled and explosives set. The hand drill is tungsten tipped for durability and it will chew three or so metres into the wall of the shaft in minutes. The drill must be drawn out slowly to see if it has gone through potch or opal. Then charges are set: as many as a dozen with long fuses to allow the miner to climb out of the shaft before they explode. Reaching the surface, the miner counts the bangs to make sure every one of them goes off. Then the blower is started up to suck out the fumes and dust.

The seasoned miner will wait fifteen or twenty minutes before going back down the shaft. And such a change has taken place! The level is now a ballroom littered with rocks, sandstone and shredded explosive fuse. The musky smell of sulphur hangs in the air from the detonation. A cautious inspection of the roof is made—if it's drummy it has to be picked down for safety.

Now the loose dirt has to be inspected before being sent up in the hoist bucket to start a mullock dump. Opal might or might not be found in the debris. Next the lead on the wall is inspected. There could be a trace of colour, a thin wafer of opal that needs the gentle gouging of the miner's pick, and this requires patient paring away of the clay for hours on end. If there is nothing to gouge more explosive holes will be drilled and fired again.

Generally a miner will spend five or six weeks in a hole before being satisfied that it is a dud and that another shaft has to be put down. Then again, miners who are on opal will stay until the last chip is taken; this could take months.

The underground miner and the open-cut miner are two entirely different operators. The open-cut miner selects a site virtually at random and drives a huge bulldozer backwards and forwards with a four metre wide blade slicing away the ground like layers of cake. This cutting away the ground to get down to the opal level often means moving thousands of tonnes of cement-hard sandstone to go down twenty metres.

Mounted on the back of the dozer is a line of tungsten ripper shoes constantly breaking up the surface that has been swept by the front blade. From a rear vision mirror the spurting furrows thrown up by the ripper

On the opal level, using rippers to break the surface

shoes are inspected. Watching the blades warns the miner when they are breaking through the last bands into the opal dirt. When it is down to opal dirt the dozer blade sweeps away the loosened rocks of sandstone to make a nice clean working face perhaps 80 metres long and 20 metres wide.

Now a row of small tungsten furrow blades is fitted behind the dozer and a picker is employed to collect the opal lifted by the furrow blades. Unfortunately the blades also cover the opal with loose dirt and many prized opals are retrieved later by noodlers.

The noodlers have to wait until the open-cuts are abandoned by miners satisfied they have all the opal to be got. Then the noodlers move in with their sieves and rakes and digging sticks, turning over the dirt, swooping down on a piece of colour. The noodlers move slowly, often on their hands and knees, searching through the soft dirt with their fingers. Many a big find has been unearthed in this way, much to the frustration of the miner who abandoned the open-cut after so much hard work.

Open-cut mining is relatively simple but it is of course much more expensive than sinking a shaft. Operating a DC6 dozer costs in excess of $100 an hour, a fortune in repairs and a frightening consumption of diesel fuel. And it's hot under that blazing sun, bouncing up and down on an uncomfortable seat all day long. The dozer is strong but some of the rocks it encounters are beyond its power and have to be blasted out with explosives.

An open-cut miner cannot work alone. One or more pickers must be hired on wages or profit-sharing schemes. A truck has to cart countless drums of fuel and water from town to the work site—and the site could be 30 kilometres on a bad road from town. When miners do get down to the opal dirt they camp on the site for a week or more until it is cleared out. There might be indications that they should go six, ten, fifteen metres deeper.

Sometimes it can cost $10 000 to find $10 of opal by open-cut mining. The open-cut miner's money might run out before the dozer gets down to the opal level. It's all a gamble—a huge one.

On the other hand the opal buyers on the field don't have these head-aches. They buy just the end result, the opal, at a fixed price without the sweat and tears that have gone into the finding. They are the low risk profit operators. Nonetheless they are the backbone of the industry, the stabilising force. Without the opal buyers there would of course be no market for the miner's opal.

Years ago a miner wrote in a diary, 'You've got to be a gambler if you're going to be a miner. And you've got to be bloody mad if you think you're ever going to win. There's a fortune here, but it'll take a few fortunes to find it.' There's many a miner today who will agree wholeheartedly with this observation.

But the place has something about it. The sounds of bedlam on the fields with the eardrum-splitting cacophony of grinding, whirring, belching, humming noises associated with opal mining. The incessant, unmelodious wail of horns and sirens signalling winches to be started, hoist drums stacked with explosives to be lowered. Hard-hatted miners pop out of holes like rabbits to the rumble of chain explosions as their explosives blast out drives, pulverising everything in the way, ripping boulders down, widening shafts. The deafening roar of nitro-pill thunders like tank fire. Then the hard hats disappear back down the shafts.

This is the new mechanised Coober Pedy with the face and bowels of the arid Gibson Desert changing daily. With gem opal fetching $8000 an ounce (30 grams). That's just a matchbox-full. But to find and uncover it, thousands of tonnes of stubborn clay and sandstone have first to be removed.

Automation has come to the opal fields. The revolutionary Calweld drill, mounted on a truck for mobility, can sink a 20 metre hole in a matter of hours—a hole wide enough for a miner to climb down. There are negative pressure conveying and separating devices that raise the dirt from the shafts, sift it, crush it and dump it on mullock heaps after spewing out the potch and precious opal.

Ultra-violet noodling machines are the rage, enclosed sheds with conveyor belts running non-stop through them, belts laden with opal dirt filled by dozers. Caterpillar earth-moving equipment builds mounds for the dozers that feed the belts that zip through the sheds where the opal pickers whip the precious gem into drums ready for the final sort. Coober Pedy's getting to be a gigantic factory geared for mass production of opal.

A whole new dimension has been introduced to the opal treasure hunt, and many more machines are on the drawing boards—sonar rock tumblers, electronic cutting machines—all specifically intended for the geographic and climatic conditions of the opal fields. Alas, the days of flinging a hemp rope down a shaft and shinning down with a humble pick and shovel have gone forever.

Some say the opal must run out. But they've been saying that for thirty years. Look out there for as far as the eye can see—it's all opal country, and still virtually untouched. The only real thing that has changed is the world demand for opal. And we've got the most and the best right here in Coober Pedy.

An open-cut opal mine. Removing thousands of tonnes of dirt to find a few ounces of precious opal

25 *Buried alive in opal*

The temptation to explore old abandoned shafts on the opal fields is an ever-present hazard faced by inexperienced fossickers, in spite of the perils of falling rock and the danger of cave-ins. But when tales of fabulous discoveries in unexpected places have whetted a person's desire for opal it can be understood why the lure of an open pit is almost irresistible.

But not so in the case of Igor Lbob (the name is a fictitious one, adopted out of respect for this Polish miner's tragic experience). The story itself is true. Igor was a Polish miner who should have known better than to climb down a rope to fossick in the depths of an abandoned shaft on the Twelve Mile Diggings.

Whatever led him to toss caution to the winds and enter the crumbling old shaft alone will never be known. In the light of what happened it could be put down to the possibility that this veteran of the opal fields could 'smell' opal down there and was prepared to take any risk to get it for himself.

It was late at night before he was missed and two of his friends went looking for him. They failed to find him and returned to town unaware that the shaft had caved in and buried him. When they resumed their search early the following day they were shocked to find miner's tools at the ragged mouth of the shaft and the fearful evidence of a cave-in: a great depth of fallen rock sealed the mouth of Igor's tomb.

With the frenzy that is a mixture of hope and despair they lunged at the rock with bare hands, hurling it blindly out of the shaft. Then other miners rushed in to tear at the fallen rock. The sun blazed down pitilessly while they worked and it was six hours before there was the least reward for their toil.

Then it came. A feeble cry percolating through tonnes of rocks. He was still alive! By some freak of fate Igor must have escaped being crushed to death.

Now his mates worked with renewed fury. As the hours passed a generator was brought up to shed light on the stark drama of men still wrestling with unrelenting rock to save a comrade's life. An air compressor was rolled up, hoses connected and rock drills roared into life. By daylight, with miners at the point of exhaustion, thirteen metres of the shaft had been cleared. Hope for the entombed man began to wane. Some who had abandoned hope said he should be left to rest in peace.

Then people came out from town with food that revived and refreshed the rescue team. They stayed to form a human chain to pass out the incarcerating rocks of Igor's tomb. A wooden table was hammered together and lowered by chains to provide a platform on which the miners could stand in case earth and stone collapsed beneath their feet.

Steadily they burrowed down deeper and deeper, bloodied hands grabbing and wrenching at lacerating rock. Men worked grimly without complaint.

Then, at last, a massive boulder was tackled by many hands and slowly, painfully, gouged from its resting place. A cry of exultation rose from the men as part of Igor's shirt, then his arm, was revealed.

But from the grave itself arose a denunciation that shocked the rescuers into frozen immobility: 'What the hell are you bastards doing? Leave me alone. You're only after my opal.'

And while not one man moved from a posture of sheer disbelief the earth beneath the platform on which they stood began to subside. It gathered momentum until it ran away like water out of a sink and Igor Lbob reached up and clawed his way out of the grave.

'My God, he's not even hurt.'

'It can't be.'

'It's a miracle.'

And while exhausted men cried out and wept in sheer relief Igor Lbob found his voice again. 'It's mine,' he gasped, opening a balled-up fist to reveal a huge opal. He swallowed dryly and went on, 'It's mine. Mine. And I've found a seam this big.' He stretched his arms wide then collapsed on the spot.

When he was carried away his two friends remained at the shaft knowing that moonlighters would make short work of robbing Igor of his find. In less than three hours they dislodged one hundred ounces of pinfire opal, worth $17 000.

Good friends though they were, they could not save Igor from what was to follow. The traumatic effects of making a fabulous discovery and being buried alive, coupled with the fear that his opal would be stolen, was too much for the veteran miner. His mind snapped and he was taken to a mental hospital in Adelaide.

26 *The million dollar fiasco*

There are tales galore of massive fortunes being made on the opal fields and it goes without saying that many of these are untrue. The most dependable stories of big finds are reported in the newspapers and then there is a population explosion on the fields until the find is worked out and things get back to normal.

But from whatever source the tales begin most of them contain a grain of truth, such as the reported finding of a million dollars' worth of opal by a small company owned by a man called Mustophe, a seasoned miner, whose party of four men hired a drilling rig and put down several holes on the Six Mile Digging. From one of these the drill brought up a quantity of precious opal. A shaft was quickly excavated and a rich seam located. The news of the find spread like bushfire and inevitably a stream of rigs and blowers came from town to the diggings. Areas adjoining the find were quickly pegged.

Sixteen metres down their shaft the men found pinfire opal in great quantity, as thick as bricks, and for hours they gouged it free and pulled it up in sacks to the surface. The same night the stone was inspected and a price was put on it by the miners. The next day it was shown to the buyers and Mustophe asked a flat million dollars for it. The buyers said no; their top offer was $190 000. The parcel was taken to a Chinese buyer who inspected it and said it was jelly opal and needed to be cleaned up to get rid of the host rock around it. He said that if this was done he would pay $210 000 for it.

There are many ways of cleaning opal and one of them is by tumbling. To Mustophe, putting the opal into a motor-driven concrete mixer seemed a good idea and he lost no time in doing so. Then he sat back dreaming about the fortune to be shared.

Several hours later the concrete mixer was stopped and the opal tipped out. Only then did the horrified Mustophe realised he had forgotten to remove the mixer's paddle blades. But by then it was too late. The blades had so battered the opal in the mixer that much of it was reduced to dust.

The salvaged opal was taken back to the buyers but after inspecting it their top price was now only $18 000. Mustophe sat in a corner of the room and wept.

One night I too missed a chance of making a worthwhile sum of money. I was living in a tin shed on the Fifteen Mile when a group of Aborigines hammered on my door clamouring to sell me a bottle containing 10 ounces of opal. They said they wanted only $200 and foolishly I refused. But that didn't discourage them from trying the other miners on the field. Finally they managed to sell their opal for $140 and off they went on a drinking spree. The next day the miner who had bought it took it to town and sold it for $3200.

Then there was the old Hungarian called Pink Eyes who had been on the fields for years, noodling through the dumps. Now and then the miners felt sorry for him and dropped, unnoticed, a small opal into his dilly-bag. One day he found a 16 ounce piece of seam opal in an open cut and sold it to the buyers for $5000. Then he quietly went around the huts of the miners who had been kind to him, leaving envelopes of money to repay their help, and left the fields never to be seen again. Pink Eyes wasn't so simple after all.

27 *Leisure time*

On the opal fields there is never enough time to do all the things you want to. Naturally the most popular pastimes have something to do with opal and nearly everyone has a wind-driven tumbling machine fixed up on the roof, or a motorised unit in a shed to clean and polish opal chips. Some miners have taken up gold and silver smithing or built exquisite models from otherwise unusable opal chippies. Some beautiful cameos, potch and colour carvings, are made by the more artistic folk.

Many hobbies and interests are the same the world over and the miners and their families collect coins and stamps, make model aeroplanes and take up photography as enthusiastically as anyone else.

In the town there are licensed Greek, Italian and Australian clubs where mixed darts championships are played and serious snooker tournaments are held. There are whist and bridge nights and always a game of poker, black-jack or manilla going.

Tom Cat Hill, a favourite lookout for photographers

Perhaps the single greatest event in Coober Pedy is the annual race day that is organised by the Progress Association as if it were the Melbourne Cup. On the day the women wear their finery and self-appointed bookies call the odds. The main street is hung with bunting and it is a holiday with a real carnival atmosphere and visitors arriving from all over Australia. There are camel and brumby and donkey events, and some of them race in two or three fields. Winners are toasted in champagne and the local traders donate trophies and prizes to the courageous jockeys.

Of lesser impact but with growing attendance are the Oodnadatta races and gymkhana held in the middle of May, with part of the proceeds going to charity. As well as horse events there are foot events in which children are encouraged to join. As the evening light falls there is the usual Saturday night shindig at the track following the day's races with music, food and liquor in abundance. The Coober Pedyites attend in force.

Many of the miners and their partners are expert shooters and go out after the plentiful wild pig and kangaroo on weekend safaris that take them as far as Oodnadatta. Those who stay at home kick a football around and get out the bat and stumps, braving the 40°C heat. Coober Pedy has a very mean cricket team that could frighten the life out of the professionals.

Residents in and around Coober Pedy welcomed the arrival of TAFE, giving their support both as teachers and students, with classes on everything from blacksmithing to Tai Chi. Nothing is uncommon on the opal fields, not even a woman standing on one leg, arms outstretched in deep meditation. As one resident said, 'You don't have to be crazy to live here, but it sure gives you a head start if you are.'

At night, Coober Pedy is not unlike a miniature city, gaily lit with flashing neons and the noisy band at the local tempting the dancers to the floor. The licensed restaurants are packed. In the main street drive-in theatre John Wayne is winning another war. Voices of a dozen nationalities sing-song along the street.

The police are always there, keeping law and order without spoiling anyone's fun, merely giving a caution or a suggestion to go home and sleep it off to those who have over-indulged.

The huge signs advertising opals for sale dwarf the bell tower of the underground church. Tourists' cameras flash as they move slowly, taking in the sights.

In their shops and cabins the opal vendors explain the characteristics of opal to their enchanted customers. The doublets, the triplets and the solids. Anything is available, from a cameo to a fossilised bone or an opalised shell!

28 *Fossils*

Mention must be made of the fossils containing precious opal which are being found on the Coober Pedy fields, for they are now fetching astronomical prices. The bones of reptiles, fish, all manner of shells and the remains of plants have been discovered quite recently.

Several of the Coober Pedy fields are noted for their pockets of opalised shells, found as deep as 30 metres. The opalisation of some of these shells means that they can be cut as solid stones. Tiffany's, jewellers on Fifth Avenue, New York, have set opalised shells in pendants and brooches with diamonds and pearls merely to complement the opal; these jewels have been shown at an exhibition to world opal buyers.

Though often thin and delicately fragile, even the poorest opalised shell is valuable as a curio, for the process of opalisation has taken over a million years.

Some of the most remarkable fossils found on the Coober Pedy field include the completely opalised skeletons of a large aquatic reptile of Cretaceous times, the plesiosaur. Measuring 1.5 metres in length, the fossilised plesiosaurs had opalised vertebrae, blade-bones and ribs. Unfortunately most of these fossils were broken up and sold for their opal content. However, there is an almost complete skeleton of a plesiosaur on display at the Australian Museum in Sydney.

In many cases the fossils are potch and have none of the colour of precious opal, but even these are snapped up by the opal buyers who know they can sell them as specimens.

The Australian opal fields over the past ten years have attracted fossil hunters from all over the world and no private collection is considered to be complete without at least a few of the more common opalised fossils. There is an abundance of opalised teeth, bones, wood, shells and belemnites to be found around the Coober Pedy, Andamooka, White Cliffs and Lightning Ridge opal fields and these common fossils, infilled and preserved by noble opal, are often of great value.

The sea shells, mussel-type bivalves and snail-like univalve fossils are very common and their value is determined by the extent of their opalisation.

Shells on the opal field can sell from $15 to $50 000 each.

Belemnites fossilised into precious opal are found as pointed pipes; they can contain the finest of harlequin patterns. Even in a poor condition, infilled with potch and colour, the belemnites are highly attractive and prized collector's pieces.

Opalised fossils are often found as cavities in the strata, preserving in detail the shapes of life-forms which existed millions of years ago during the Cretaceous period.

Finding an opalised fossil is a bonus for the professional miner intent on following a lead. It is the unexpected prize and often whole pockets of shells are discovered nearby. Broken or partly filled shells of opal are cut into solid stones but intact fossils are left in their natural condition, fetching far more money for their uniqueness.

29 *The art of lapidary*

Comparable to the pleasure of finding opal is the tremendous satisfaction of converting uninteresting, badly-shaped and often lustreless stones into beautiful baroque free-form gems ready for setting. This is the art of lapidary, made easy by the use of tumblers which are miniature grinding mills that convert material in the rough into highly polished gem stones.

Tumbling and polishing stones is a recent development in Australia that is becoming extremely popular with the hobbyist and many different tumblers are readily available. A reliable machine can be bought inexpensively and can be operated in the garage or home workshop.

Basically a tumbler is a motor that drives two parallel shafts on which drums or barrels rotate at slow speeds. The barrels contain a small amount of water and several grades of silicon carbide, introduced over a period of one week to ten days. As much as 5 kilograms of stone can be polished in a single operation, with the tumbler acting in much the same way as the sand-wearing water currents to which beach and stream pebbles are subjected.

For use in closely populated areas where noise has to be controlled, several varieties of rubber drums, barrels and tumblers with ball-bearing shafts have been devised. This is quite important as a tumbler has to run 24 hours a day for satisfactory results.

Most tumblers come complete with instructions for maintenance and for polishing stones. The Wessex Impex, an English machine available at most lapidary shops, is a technically advanced concept inasmuch as up to five barrels at a time can be operated by one motor. This high-speed tumbler has a multidrive unit for speed reduction with raised and lower bearings, as low speed has to be employed in the final polishing of stones. As well as opals, tumblers can polish abalone shell, marble, obsidian, quartz, tigereye, agates and a number of other materials.

Tumbling, however, is only one aspect of the art of lapidary, though perhaps it is the most important one. On the opal fields in areas where there is no electricity the miners rig up wind-driven tumblers. These are propeller-driven shafts fixed to a drum that revolves on rods fitted with bearings.

The lapidary who has the use of a shed or garage at home can gradually build up a workshop item by item. A grinder with a rough and smooth, water-cooled wheel is essential in the shaping of stones and grinding away of sandstone and other host material. The grinder can be improvised to carry wheels of varying grits mounted on a single shaft, for a really harsh abrasive will wear a stone away and with opal at $10 to $500 a carat this can be an expensive loss.

The dedicated lapidary will soon learn the need for a diamond saw with a 12 centimetre blade which will slice the opal into manageable stones, triplets and doublets. The best diamond saw is one with varying speeds and a foot pressure switch that leaves the hands free to work. A good diamond saw will slice a nugget stone into many triplet wafers with very little waste. It will face a stone to show its best cutting angles and its colour highlights. It will expose sandstone and crazing.

Top priority in any workshop is good lighting. Imperfections in stones are often not noticeable in poor light. Lights should be over every machine and shielded so as not to glare into the eyes. Many a good stone has been ruined because a good light wasn't available to study its flaws or to show its best face for cutting on a diamond saw.

Many home workshops have all of the machinery operating on a single shaft and run off one motor. This is not wise even if it is the cheapest arrangement. It can be disturbing to say the least to be concentrating on shaping a stone on a wheel while a diamond saw blade hums dangerously close by. Add to this the racket of slapping grinder belts, a tumbler filled with rocks bouncing merrily only centimetres away—it's plain lunacy.

So, with the machinery properly installed on suitable work benches, two separate areas need to be left clear. One is for sorting stones into sizes, standards and progress of polishing. A number of glass jars half-filled with water make excellent containers. The water in the jars cushions the stones, keeps them free of dust and grit and shows their best colours, while making different grades of material easily recognisable.

The second area set aside is for dopping stones preparatory to grinding. The practice of holding a stone between two fingers against a high-speed carborundum wheel generally results in both fingers being ground as the stone flies at great speed through the air to smash to pieces against some solid object. Obviously this painful and expensive way of grinding stone is not to be encouraged.

A dop stick must be used. This is a pencil-thick stick, five centimetres long, to which the stone is cemented with wax heated on a spirit lamp. The stone is fixed firmly and can be turned safely on a wheel or a lap and cut.

Lapidary work is an acquired skill and it would be unthinkable to experiment on precious gem opals. With so much potch available which is worked in the same manner as good opal, mistakes can be made with little expense. Working with precious opal, as little as a single turn of a grinding wheel can burn away a splendid veneer of beautiful colour.

When the workshop is complete all kinds of stones: agates, thunder eggs, moonstones and jaspers, can be ground and polished along with the princely opal.

30 *Classing and sorting*

'How can I find out what an opal is worth?' is a question asked by just about everyone fascinated by opal. The classing and grading of opal can be learnt as soon as you gain practical experience. This is interesting work and essential if the best price is to be obtained when selling a parcel.

Opal is sorted into grades known as firsts, seconds and thirds, then chippies and potch and colour. Before a parcel of opal can be graded the colours must be exposed. This is done with a pair of tungsten-tipped snips that pinch away the host rock. Only a tiny fragment of skin is removed so that no gem material is wasted.

All solid stones in the parcel are set aside initially and materials that can be cut into attractive doublets and triplets are graded according to their display of colour and depth; these are put into bottles for later attention. The real value in any parcel lies in the solids and these have to be classed individually.

Classing opal calls for patience if a fine display of colour is to be exposed in a stone, just enough colour for a buyer to see its quality and measure its potential as a cutter. The material has to be shown to its best advantage and to reveal any possible bad points such as a deep sandspot, a scum or smoky film.

Snipping is important. Too much must not be cut away. Pressure in the wrong place can crush the stone, crack it or make faults and blemishes which lower the value.

Some stones only have to be faced to show an area of display while others have to be cut to get rid of adhering sandstone. Do not develop a snipping mania, for a sizeable stone can soon be reduced to a fraction of its original size.

Having processed a parcel in a workman-like style it is then sorted into class. Any eye can pick out an exceptional stone and make it a 'first'. Sorting low grade potch and colour is just as obvious. Good colour is so-called not only for its beauty and brightness but because it runs true: in a straight bar, or as magically intermixing colours over the entire face of a stone. Bad colour is dull or streaky or it runs out and potch comes in.

A good stone displays patches of reds and gold and orange and blues and green. No two stones are alike. There are the flash, the fire, the flame and the elusive 'pinpoint'. Again there is the stone flooded with a number of colours or the one with varying colours that change at the slightest movement from crimson to brilliant green and then to vivid orange. Imprisoned in the stone are the laws of light diffraction and the elements of colour. The amazing varieties of hues, the designs and shapes that opals take are endless.

Beauty being in the eye of the beholder, how best to class these gems according to their beauty, variety, weight, size, pattern and colour? It is a constant battle of wits between buyer and seller, but the market is all on the seller's side.

Having selected the best and put them aside as firsts, it's easy to sort those of medium quality. The remainder—those with poor colour, sand spots or untrue colours—are the thirds. And in the snipping area there is a pile of chips that can be cleaned and sold by the ounce. Now the parcel is ready to be sold and mentally a price is put on it, reckoned by what similar material is fetching. Perhaps one or two really excellent stones will be put aside for polishing by a professional lapidary.

31 *Gem merchants and jewellers*

It is so easy to ruin a precious opal by not understanding its characteristics and qualities. Often in removing the imprisoning potch to free the colours the amateur lapidary grinds away a whole face of colour.

A rich gem, hidden for millions of years in Australia's scorching desert, discovered by the lone miner's pick, needs to be brought to life by a skilled artisan.

The gem merchants Altmann and Cherney have marketed for many years most of the important opals found in Australia. They have cut and supplied opals to royalty and celebrities, museums and jewellers throughout the world. In their Melbourne showrooms can be seen an outstanding range of red and green fire opals from Andamooka and Coober Pedy: the noble black opal from Lightning Ridge, expensive colourful opal doublets and triplets, opal matrix, unusual carved opals, collector's and investment stones cut and

The Umoona mine, under Aboriginal control, includes large showrooms where opal from the mine can be purchased

polished in their own workshops. Here the glorious *Olympic Australis* can be viewed by appointment. Found on the opal field of Coober Pedy at the Eight Mile Diggings in 1956, just in time for the Melbourne Olympic Games, it took its name partly in their honour and partly for the flashing lights of the Aurora Australis, the southern polar lights which its myriad brilliant sparkles resemble.

Only an artist can bring out the best colours and patterns in an opal. And a skilled artisan is needed to design an appropriate setting that will do it justice. There are many self-taught lapidaries who claim proudly to have cut and polished first class gem material on grinding wheels. But at what cost? Heaven only knows what precious opal has been ground to dust in their inexperienced hands. It's like a butcher attempting heart surgery; the operation is successful but the patient dies. So it is with precious opal. It takes shape but the colour melts away, killed by the rough, tearing carborundum wheel.

The cutting and polishing of gem quality opal should be left to the experts. But who are the experts? Generally the local jeweller is not an opal specialist but a retailer of gem stones who knows little about opal cutting. There are opal specialists, merchants who deal almost exclusively in opal, such as Percy Marks in Sydney and others who have spent years evaluating and cutting opal. Such reputable opal specialists can easily be found for they are listed in various directories.

A very high code of ethics is maintained by the established opal merchants and cutters. They will not mutilate a stone or give false valuations. They have built their reputations through many years of handling opals worth millions of dollars.

The gem merchants employ the very best cutters, top artists who command top money for cutting quality stone. Unlike general lapidaries who cut any and every stone, these cutters only touch opal.

So, if an opal is good enough, have it cut by the best, even if it does cost a lot more than the amateur at the local rock club would charge. The same policy applies in buying opal, especially opal bought as an investment. Go to the specialist, an opal merchant.

32 *Selling your opal*

Equally as important as finding opal is selling opal and now is the time to show the parcel to buyers. There are always plenty in Coober Pedy.

Often as many as thirty Chinese buyers stay at the Opal Inn Motel in Coober Pedy; they will buy almost everything on offer, from $10 an ounce chippies to solids worth thousands. They sit or stand inside their doorways, patient and smiling and always immaculately dressed. Some pass the time playing mah-jong, slapping down the tiles as they wait for the miners to bring along their parcels.

All opal has a price, even potch and colour as well as common grey. Some buyers handle as much as 30 000 grams of this material a day.

In the buyer's room, the opal is tipped onto a black plastic cloth, picked up, and inspected under a strong light. Very quickly it is sorted into heaps and then the bargaining begins. The miner seldom gets the price he asks. The eagle-eyed buyer fingers the stones and makes an offer.

Gem material is sold at so much a carat and other classes at so much per gram. A gram of pure opal is just 5 carats. Seam opal is particularly good to sell by weight for the colour may run right through its thickness.

Of course, a real gemstone of considerable size cannot be subject to run-of-the-mill prices. Such gems are classed 'beyond price' and are sold by negotiation. Sometimes several buyers will pool their money to purchase an especially outstanding gemstone.

In selling opal it is colour, size and 'solidness' that count, and particularly pattern. Of all the patterns the magic of the harlequin is the most prized. The flame stone in which, as you slowly turn it, a flash of red sweeps over the face like a raging bushfire is the most valuable colouring, just as harlequin is the most prized pattern.

Many rich overseas buyers are currently visiting the opal fields, for opal is becoming a better investment than gold or diamonds. The huge prices these buyers are prepared to pay seem unreal.

Apart from the Chinese buyers there are other buyers living permanently in and around Coober Pedy. All of these have signs outside their offices and homes advertising that they buy opal at the best prices.

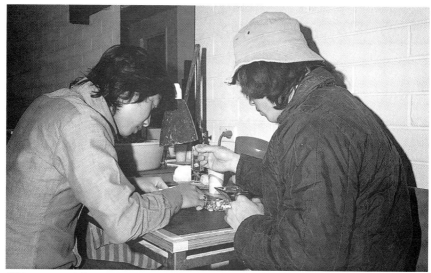

Chinese opal buyers inspecting a parcel of opal

The city buyers from Sydney, Melbourne and Adelaide come to Coober Pedy regularly, some every two weeks. They rent rooms at the motels and usually are prepared to pay more for the opal they buy to get a few good parcels together quickly.

The miner has an open market. The tourists stopping a few days can return the cost of their trip by purchasing a few investment stones. Having opal in the pocket is as good as having money in the bank.

Coober Pedy is only one market for selling opal. Opal dealers and gem merchants in every city are only too pleased to have a look at a parcel. In Adelaide alone there are over two hundred opal buyers, many of them listed in the telephone directory. It isn't hard to sell opal. A small advertisement in a newspaper often brings many enquiries.

The wrong time to sell opal is of course in desperation. When you have to sell anything quickly the price always drops. No worthwhile parcel of opal ever goes begging, there is always a buyer at the right price. It's just a matter of shopping around until its true value is offered.

33 *Investing in opal*

The question of just what is a fair price for a particular piece of opal and its investment potential has been the topic of much journalism throughout the world recently with opals vying in value with investment diamonds.

As with all precious gem stones, opal sells by carat weight for cut stones and by the gram in the rough. A carat can range in value from $3 to $1000 depending on its design and play of colours. In good black opal the sky's the limit.

Black opals from Lightning Ridge and Mintabie are the most valuable materials, especially if they are harlequin or red or blue fire opal. This material sells for $6000 and upwards a carat. The demand for good black opal is far in excess of supply and Australian black opal is renowned all over the world for its colours and investment value.

The semi-black variety of opal comes from every field in Australia and ranges from the dark grey opal found at Coober Pedy to the precious black boulder opal of Queensland. Equally as scarce as true black opal, black boulder is extremely popular and sells at prices from $400 to $3000 a carat.

In buying a stone for investment the type of stone, its size and shape, its brilliance, pattern and colour all have to be taken into consideration. Brilliance is the main factor in the visual appeal of opal, but supply and demand also condition its price. A small 5 carat white-base Coober Pedy opal with a star pattern, because of its rarity, could be as valuable as the finest black harlequin. Only a few star opals have been found in Australia.

Opals can be valued on a three-point basis of colour, pattern and natural formation; from these prime aspects opal values can be ascertained. With even a basic knowledge of opal, fire patterns and natural formations, opal can be appraised quite easily. Once visual appeal is established in a type of opal, be it crystal, jelly, boulder, seam, vertical or matrix, the next consideration is the finish of the stone. Opals are sold as solids, doublets and triplets. Obviously solids are worth more because they are wholly opal. High-domed doublets are ranked next, then triplets, last are flat-faced doublets.

The oval-shaped opal is in greater demand than the irregular freeform and domed stones are preferred to flat ones. The expensive black and the fine crystal are rarely cut to calibrated size but lesser opal is cut to square, oval and oblong sizes to fit standard sized jewellery fittings.

So the best shape and size is determined, but colour play now conditions the price of the stone. In the scale of colours red is most popular, followed by oranges, greens then blues. A combination of colours providing classic contrasts raises the price of the stone. While red is in demand the brilliance of colour is extremely important. A poor red is not worth as much as a brilliant blue. The perfect investment stone then is a large oval-shaped brilliant red, especially if it has a black base.

The investor in opal is strongly advised only to buy cut stones. Opals in the rough are a risk as they may have concealed faults, cracking, sand spots or be subject to crazing. Only the experienced eye of the cutter can tell a good rough opal from a bad one. In buying a cut stone all of its faults are apparent and its best appeal has been brought out by the cutter.

There can be no scale of established charges for opal as prices rise at a staggering rate. Black opal sold for £50 in 1925 resold for $24 000 in 1994. A 17-carat red on white base Coober Pedy stone that sold for $190 in 1963 was revalued in 1994 at $2000.

Even the small investor can make money in opal. It is useless investing now in a stone worth less than $500 on today's market, for those stones would have been worth less than a hundred dollars ten years ago and have reached their top price. But stones now available for more than $500 will escalate considerably over the next few years. And if the yield of opal diminishes, these investment stones will rocket in price. There is every indication of a shortage in opal occurring if new fields are not quickly established, for Coober Pedy, Andamooka and Lightning Ridge are supplying the bulk of world opal.

The investor able to go out to the opal fields can buy good grade parcels of opal at fair prices in the rough but it is a considerable gamble. All reasonably valued parcels of opal have a ready sale through established buyers who visit the fields regularly. The opal miner is not desperate to sell his material and there is no such thing as bargain opal. It is a case of getting exactly what you pay for. If a parcel of opal is cheap it is either because its grade is low or because the material is faulty.

The glut of low grade rough opal ranging from $5 a piece potch and colour to $50 low-grade grey opal is feeding the lapidary shops. If it is cheap enough to be ground away by an amateur lapidary on the wheel it will never make investment material. It is quality that counts in investment and not quantity. Huge parcels of low grade opal are available on the fields and that is where this material should stay! Rising prices being commanded by good grade material means no reputable buyer is interested in low grade opal.

As with any investment, opal should only be purchased from a reputable gem merchant who guarantees the material is of a specific quality. Presentation cases of specially selected investment stones are on sale at prices ranging from $2000. These are numbered, are of the finest quality, and carry a certificate of value for insurance purposes.

34 *A tourist development survey*

The Publicity and Design Services branch of the South Australian Premier's Department has kindly provided the following information in a survey that examines the nature of existing tourist activity in the Far North of South Australia and provides the basis for an understanding of the inter-relationship of factors which determine the present characteristics of tourism in this area.

Principal features of the region

The region generally recognised as the Far North of South Australia comprises approximately three-quarters of the total area of the state. It extends approximately 700 kilometres from north to south and approximately 1150 kilometres from east to west and includes most of the unincorporated areas of South Australia.

The borders of Western Australia, Queensland, New South Wales and the Northern Territory define the western, eastern and northern boundaries of the region, while the southern boundary adjoins the Eyre Peninsula, Flinders Ranges and Riverland Tourist regions of South Australia.

The present population of the Far North region is estimated to be 19 000 or approximately one per cent of the population of the State. The largest towns are Coober Pedy (permanent population 2300), Andamooka (500), Maree (350) and Oodnadatta (200). Other centres of population are Kingoonya, Tarcoola and the townships along the Barrier Highway to Broken Hill.

Major transport routes in the region include the Stuart Highway, Birdsville Track, Strzelecki Track, Maree-Oodnadatta road, Barrier Highway, the Indian Pacific railway and the Central Australian railway.

Climate and physical environment

The Far North region receives a low erratic rainfall ranging from 250 mm per year along the margins of the Flinders Ranges to less than 100 mm per year in the Lake Eyre Basin. In the western part of the region the average annual rainfall varies from 200 mm on the Nullarbor Plain to 150 mm in the

Musgrave Ranges. There is an extreme annual and seasonal variability in rainfall throughout the region.

The region experiences extremely hot summer periods and mild to warm winters. In the summer months of December–January the mean monthly maximum ranges from 32–38°C and the mean monthly minimum during winter ranges from 3–6°C. The large seasonal and daily fluctuations in temperature result from extreme radiation, clear skies, low humidity and isolation from the sea.

Although the Far North region is characterised by the overall diversity of its landscapes it includes four major physiographic landforms:

the mountainous deserts which include the Musgrave, Everard, Gawler and Olary Ranges.

the shield deserts of the western part of the region including the Great Victoria Desert and the Nullarbor Plain.

the extensive low-lying salt plains, the largest of which are Lakes Eyre, Torrens, Gairdner and Frome.

the sand deserts north of Lake Eyre and south of the Musgrave Ranges of which the Simpson Desert is the most prominent.

Scenic and recreational attractions
Coober Pedy is a thriving urban centre with a population fluctuating between 1800 and 2300, surrounded by intensive open cut mining operations extending 40 kilometres from the town centre. The town has developed in an informal haphazard manner and its colourful frontier way of life has gained international recognition. It is anticipated that Coober Pedy will continue its rapid expansion and become the provincial centre of the central and western segments of the Far North region.

A recreation area for Coober Pedy residents, Lake Phillipson, lies 70 kilometres from the town. A profuse growth of tea tree, coolabah and spear grass covers the flood plains of the Long, Mabel and Woorang creeks which drain into the lake from the north. Access is through a picturesque landscape of bright red sand dunes and mulga.

Although there has been an observed increase in visitor penetration to this region over recent years, particularly focusing on Coober Pedy, the total number of travellers involved remains extremely low when compared to visitor levels elsewhere in the state.

Profile of visitors to the region
The characteristics of visitors to the Far North region reflect a higher than average proportion of retired and semi-retired people and younger age groups.

In general, visitors can be identified as travellers in transit (particularly on the Stuart Highway), those people touring the area over a prolonged period and visitors on organised tours of up to two weeks.

Due to the close association between the Far North of South Australia and the wider concept of Central Australia, visitors to the region are drawn from all States of Australia, with the greatest proportions from South Australia and Victoria.

To a significant extent Adelaide is still recognised as the gateway to Central Australia.

Seasonality

High summer temperatures have led to extreme seasonal variations in the number of visitors to the region.

Nearly all visitor activity occurs during the period March-November with the most popular months being April-September and particularly school holiday periods.

Some indicators of the volume of tourism in the region

The principal operators involved in scheduled four-wheel drive safari tours to the region are Desert Trek Australia Pty Ltd, Transcontinental Safaris, and Rover Charter Tours. Each enterprise was established in Adelaide during the mid 1960s.

Although each operation undertakes a range of safaris to different areas and in addition benefits from special interest charter work, the main focus of safari tours is the north-east sector and particularly the Birdsville Track and Innamincka area.

The number of visitors to the region travelling in private cars is comparatively small. Private travellers are predominantly confined to the main roads in the area.

The South Australian Government Tourist Bureau does not actively encourage travel by private motor vehicle to the Far North region. However a comprehensive range of printed information on four-wheel drive safari and coach trips to the region is available through its offices in Adelaide, Melbourne and Sydney.

Summary and conclusions

The remarkable diversity of landscape in the Far North and its specific unique attractions constitute an excellent resource for tourist development.

Previously the region's lack of facilities and climatic extremes somewhat restricted the number of visitors when compared to tourist levels elsewhere in the state. With good roads and airconditioned comfort in coaches and accommodation it is anticipated that the existing patterns of tourism in the

*The landmark Big Winch above the town centre, where opal can be
purchased at low field prices*

region will change significantly in the foreseeable future.

As the largest population centre in the region, the opal town of Coober
Pedy will continue to play an important role in the provision of visitor facilities and the component of its local economic base concerned with the tourist
industry will grow substantially.

Visitors to the region can be identified as transit travellers, those touring
the area over a long period, organised four-wheel-drive safaris and coach
tour groups. Most visitor activity occurs from April to September.

In recent years improved road conditions have allowed the use of
conventional cars by visitors to the region, where previously below
average conditions minimised their use; this was recognised as being the
major constraint on the growth of tourism.

The exploration and finds of opals on new fields will attract more miners
to Coober Pedy, increasing the population. Currently good opal on established fields is scarce and fetching high prices, demand exceeding supply.

35 *Various types of opal*

Every type of opal has special characteristics. This guide will help you recognise different types.

Composition Hydrated silica, $SiO_2.nH_2O$ (silicon dioxide).
Hardness 5½ to 6½ on the Mohs scale.
Fracture Conchoidal.
Lustre Vitreous.

Amber opal Opal having an amber or golden body colour.
Black opal Precious opal with a dark to black background, which accentuates the display of colours in the stone.
Boulder opal Precious opal found in cracks and cavities in boulders of ironstone and cut with a boulder base.
Cherry opal Precious opal in which a flash predominates over a cherry-red base.
Crystal opal Transparent opal with flowing liquid colour. Only type of opal which can be facetted, resulting in multi-dimensional colour display.
Fire opal Opal containing small but brilliant pin-spots of colour.
Flame opal Precious opal in which the colour shows in red bands or streaks like flickering flames.
Flash opal Opal with sudden flashes of brilliant colours.
Floaters Mineral traces found lying loose on surface.
Harlequin opal Opal containing patches of changing colours.
Heliotrope A purple colour.
Hydrophane Opal that becomes more transparent in water.
Jelly opal A variety of high translucency and weak colour play.
Milk opal Opal with brilliant colouring on white milky background.
Mineral jelly A naturally occurring form of silica gel.
Moss opal Common opal with dendritic inclusions.
Nobbies Rounded nodular pieces of opal.
Opalite A green or yellow common opal.
Opal matrix Ironstone with thin veins or flecks of precious opal.

Painted lady Rock coated or impregnated with opal.

Pineapples Opal masses formed in cavities, reminiscent of small pine-apples.

Pipe opal Precious opal found in tubular channels in the sandstone.

Potch A common opal found with precious opal. Valueless as a gemstone but is used for backing opal doublets and triplets.

Potch and colour Pieces of common opal showing traces of colour.

Precious opal A variety of opal which is of value on account of its irides-cent colours.

Resin opal A variety similar to wax or pitch opal.

Seam opal Opal which has formed in seams, cracks or fissures in the rocks.

Striped opal Opal running in bands with potch.

Yowah nuts Small nodules of volcanic ironstone occasionally containing precious opal, found only in north-west Queensland.

36 *Terminology*

What are mullock and angel stone, cabochons and conglomerate, gibbers and troglodytes, potch and colour, a slip or a slide? Where is a squibby level, a vertical silcrete? These are, essentially, the opal miners' language, the patter as men rub shoulders and talk in the pubs and clubs of the opal fields about their 'show'.

Alluvial opal Opal found usually on the surface of the ground that has eroded from host rocks. Usually crazed and valueless, but a very important indication of an outcrop or opal in the shallows.

Angel stone Opalised concretions of sandstone. Thin veneers of opaline silica that have a value as a specimen.

Bulldust Red to yellow silts. Peppery. Basal portion of the Bulldog Shale beneath the mud.

Cabochon A shaped opal with a domed surface and a flat back. The most preferable of cut opals. Most opal is cut in this fashion if thickness allows, providing a greater play of colour.

Colour the rainbow hues and displays in precious opal.

Common opal, potch, hyalite Colourless but often the same texture as precious opal. Sometimes used as backing behind thin opal. Can be black, red, yellow or white. It has no value.

Conglomerate Boulders, granules, composition, mixture, cemented as one. Often coarse grained sedimentary rock that can contain opal silica.

Crazed or cracky opal Often alluvial opal. Opal with hairline fractures that open as it dries out, often caused by the use of explosives. Crazed opal can slowly disintegrate to a sugary or powder form, rendering it valueless.

Doublet A layer of precious opal fixed to a natural or an artificial face to give it strength and thickness, enabling otherwise uselessly thin precious opal to be used.

Dugout A home below the ground. Excavated rooms below the surface where temperatures are moderate; unlike surface homes, dugouts are not so susceptible to heat and dust storms.

False level A level that can contain opal. A kopi mud interface that in the past has deceived miners into believing it to be a true level. Further investigation, often by other miners at some later date, may reveal a deeper, rich main level. An example is the Olympic field where in 1956 the rich prize of the *Olympic Australis* was found; this single stone is now valued at over $12 million.

Floaters Opal eroded and separated from original host rock. Often bleached and crazed due to exposure. Found in dry creeks and gullies and close to mesas or scarps from where they have leached. Often a good guide to opal outcrops.

Gibbers Silcrete and quartzite pebbles and boulders. Reddish brown and weathershined. Found everywhere in and around Coober Pedy, both above and below the ground. Colour-stained by surface iron oxides.

Gilson opal Synthetic opal, originally made in Switzerland. Has fixed colours without play. Very costly to produce and can be recognised when put against true opal.

Grey billy Cemented silcrete. Extremely hard and dense. Sometimes called 'shincracker'. Generally grey or greenish in colour. Often in a level or slide where opal is to be found.

Ironstone band Often a horizontal layer of limonite and goethite within sandstone. Opal can be found within the ironstone band or in horizontal cracks above and below it. The presence of an ironstone band is a good indicator of opal. It can form both a false and a main level or several levels.

Kopi Grey silty clay sometimes called sandstone. Really, kopi is fine grained gypsum. Colour depends on weathering and bleaching.

Level Where opal is found, alternately called the 'true' or the 'main' level where concentrations of gypsum/kopi, iron oxides, and alumite run in a near horizontal. Perfect conditions for an opal level that may be subject to slips or faults. To be followed for other seams or pockets of precious opal.

Mud Dark, often moist bulldog shale claystone resting beneath coloured sandstone. Consolidated clays and silts.

Noodling Searching for precious opal that has been overlooked by miners on dumps and in open cuts. Professional noodling machines operate on the fields. Fossickers and tourists use fine screened sieves. Often good finds are made. Permission *must* be obtained before entering upon or noodling on any active mine or opal cut. Miners are usually tolerant of noodlers.

Opal Hydrates of silica ($SiO_2.nH_2O$); scientific name, opaline silica. Opal that does not contain any colour is called potch by the miners. The many colour definitions of opal include pinfire, harlequin, fiery floral, crystal, chequerboard and white milk. Some Australian fields produce matrix and boulder opal.

Opal triplet A thin layer of precious opal that is sandwiched between a clear domed crystal or plastic face and a base of natural or artificial opaque material. An opal triplet can be very valuable.

Painted lady Usually a quartzite boulder containing a vein or face of opal, valuable as a specimen. More commonly found on the Andamooka opal fields. Often embellished with hand painted artwork and sold to tourists.

Pipe opal Opalised fossil of a belemnite. Valuable as a specimen but can be cut into small stones.

Potch Valueless opal. Sometimes there are traces of colour; called potch and colour, this has a low value. Sometimes used to back a doublet or a triplet. It comes in a variety of colours. When potch is found underground, often in thick seams, it can pinch down to narrow seams of precious opal.

Seam opal A level or bed of opal formed in a horizontal or near horizontal structure. Sometimes a mixture of potch and precious opal. At Coober Pedy there can be many levels down to a final bottom level.

Shell opal Fossil shells that have opalised, some can be solid opals, others are skins with the outer layer opalised, the inner mud-filled before opalisation. Opal shells are highly prized for both their show of colour and their fossilisation.

Silcrete Quartz, chalcedony and opaline silica. Grey billy silcrete. A very hard rock or jasper common to the opal fields.

Slip or Slide A ground fault that may displace a level. Often opal is found in these conditions and in joints. Whole levels can slip or slide steeply, forming another level.

Squibby level A level that may contain small traces of opal. Not a definite level, generally of limited lateral extent. A false level that sometimes promises a main level at a deeper depth.

Troglodyte Defined in dictionaries as a cave dweller. In Coober Pedy a troglodyte is a person who lives in an underground dugout.

Trace Small pieces of opal found in a level or a vertical or brought up from underground by a mining drill. A miner will sink a shaft if good enough opal traces are found and the approximate depth can be ascertained by measuring drill coring.

Tamping The seating of explosive plugs in drilled holes.

Verticals Joints, steeply dipping, generally infilled with gypsum, iron oxide or opal. Generally little indication of where a vertical may be found.

37 Caring for opal

When opal jewellery is not being worn keep it in a dark place, a drawer or a box, away from sun or harsh lights that can colour-fade it. Never allow opal to come in contact with oils and perfumes, which can damage the stone and fade the colour too, and never wash any opal—solids, doublets or triplets—with any kind of detergent or abrasive material.

In time, however, even the best kept opal will require cleaning, which can be done quite easily. A little vinegar in water applied with a toothbrush will remove surface dirt, while small scratches on the face of an opal can be removed and its brilliance restored by applying toothpaste to a soft cloth and rubbing the surface. Toothpaste is a very gentle cutting agent which will not harm the stone.

Do not use any other type of cleaner, including jewellery cleaner, to clean an opal as many of these have a spirit base that will penetrate the stone and dull the colour.

Any competent lapadist can buff and repolish a solid opal without removing it from a setting. Often this can be done while you wait as it only takes a few minutes and costs very little. If you have any qualms, of course, take your stone to a jeweller who specialises in opal. Repolishing an opal restores its original beauty. Opal doublets are more difficult to deal with— you can only have scratches removed as the opal is encased with either a plastic or crystal capping.

37 *In conclusion*

It is impossible to estimate how many millions of dollars have been mined in opal in Coober Pedy since it was first found in 1915, eighty years ago, as there are no production returns submitted by miners to the Department of Mines and Energy, as is required for all other mineral finds, and certainly the Taxation Department has never been, nor will be able to, assess what was found and how much it sold for. Obviously, in many cases where statements have been lodged, the amount of rough and cut opal sold commercially or privately is grossly understated.

During the period 1976–1977 the understated value of opal production from Coober Pedy was in the region of $30 million, judging by a formula based on the capital investment of mining equipment operating on the field, the cost of living per person, new businesses, buildings and home improvements. Use of this rough yardstick provides these production estimates: 1967 to 1970: $21 million, 1971 to 1977: $141 million, 1978 to 1990: $292 million, total production from 1967 to 1990: $454 million approximately.

These figures include what is called a bonanza factor, an assumption that one miner in every hundred makes a larger than average find of opal a year. $100 000 is considered to be a bonanza find. But if 2 or 5 per cent of miners annually have a bonanza strike, then production figures based on the formula referred to above are far from accurate. And the bonanza factor fixed at $100 000 isn't outstanding inasmuch as strikes of $500 000 are not uncommon.

So why, in hard times, with so much unemployment, hasn't there been a population explosion in Coober Pedy? After all, the quality of life on this opal field has vastly improved, now providing every modern amenity. The town boasts a police station staffed by 16 officers, a hospital, ambulance service, school, airport, community health centre, golf club, Olympic swimming pool, hotels and motels and caravan parks, post office and supermarket and general stores. There is a daily bus service to Adelaide, the Coober Pedy community newspaper, outback tours, underground bookshop, Catacomb and other churches of many denominations, the Greek, Italian and Australian clubs, service stations, Royal Flying Doctor Service, a Mines

Rescue Squad, residents' association, Aboriginal Welfare, CES offices and much, much more. A veritable city in a desert. Radio and television, Keno and X-lotto. . . what more could one ask for?

What keeps the population down? Perhaps the stories of violence and insecurity, tales of pathos, heartbreak and harsh climatic conditions. Or the isolation and the enervating climate.

Less than 25 per cent of the population mines for opal. Catering for the tourists, a fluctuating industry, provides employment for quite a number of residents. On the whole, the Coober Pedyites are industrious, hard working people with great community pride and spirit. They had to be to build a spectacular city out in the land of the gibbers.

Notwithstanding, only one thing can bring the venturesome to this out-back town and that is a new huge opal strike on a hitherto unrecognised field. Recently the *Coober Pedy Times* headlined on its front page: 'Any opal? Coober Pedy and the world have an opal shortage. We need more miners. . . People are still finding opal. It has not run out. There is still a lot of virgin country out there that could possibly hold the rich bonanzas we are all looking for. Coober Pedy miners must make a concentrated effort to prospect for these fields. What we need is another Olympic or 15 Mile. The market demand for opal is very strong.'

And this supported by the Department of Mines and Energy. In their publication *Opal: South Australian Gemstone,* on page 96 under Prospecting, they state, 'Large areas of the Coober Pedy precious stones field are prospective for opal but known opal fields occupy only a small proportion of the field. Generally, all areas of deeply weathered Bulldog Shale west of the Stuart Range escarpment have potential, although the type of weathered profile found in opal fields is an exploration guide for new areas. A particularly prospective area extends from Kenda Flat and Hans Peak westward along a plateau to Mars.' They go on to say, 'To locate new fields, more exploratory drilling is required than in the past.'

To date these areas have not been investigated. Perhaps here are rich bonanzas waiting to be discovered!

In saying Coober Pedy has every modern amenity, that isn't to say this outback frontier has lost its natural charm and challenge. The township is a facade and less than a kilometre away rests the inhospitable desert region. Aside from the mullock dumps and mechanised machinery, it is the same land that the first opal miners looked out over in 1915. The same ranges, the same lure that quickens the spirit and makes you want to drive a pick into virgin ground in search for that magnificent gem that is OPAL.

Index